Intellectual Capital

Jay Chatzkel

T0323758

- Fast track route to understanding and managing intellectual capital

- Covers the key areas of intellectual capital, from value-adding intellectual capital programmes and value capture to finding the 'hook' and setting up measures

- Examples and lessons from some of the world's most successful businesses, including Dow Chemical, Rockwell International, Clarica, and Buckman Labs, and ideas from the smartest thinkers, including Karl Erik Sveiby, Baruch Lev, Hubert Saint-Onge, Patrick Sullivan, Goran Roos and Leif Edvinsson

- Includes a glossary of key concepts and a comprehensive resources guide

>>EXPRESS EXEC.COM<<

essential management thinking at your fingertips

Copyright © Capstone Publishing 2002

The right of Jay Chatzkel to be identified as the author of this work has been
asserted in accordance with the Copyright, Designs and Patents Act 1988

First published 2002 by
Capstone Publishing (A Wiley Company)
8 Newtec Place
Magdalen Road
Oxford OX4 1RE
United Kingdom
http://www.capstoneideas.com

CIP catalogue records for this book are available from the British Library and the
US Library of Congress

ISBN 1-84112-256-4

This book is printed on acid-free paper

Substantial discounts on bulk quantities of Capstone books are available
to corporations, professional associations and other organizations. Please
contact Capstone for more details on +44 (0)1865 798 623 or (fax) +44
(0)1865 240 941 or (e-mail) info@wiley-capstone.co.uk

Contents

Introduction to ExpressExec

ExpressExec is 3 million words of the latest management thinking compiled into 10 modules. Each module contains 10 individual titles forming a comprehensive resource of current business practice written by leading practitioners in their field. From brand management to balanced scorecard, ExpressExec enables you to grasp the key concepts behind each subject and implement the theory immediately. Each of the 100 titles is available in print and electronic formats.

Through the ExpressExec.com Website you will discover that you can access the complete resource in a number of ways:

» printed books or e-books;
» e-content – PDF or XML (for licensed syndication) adding value to an intranet or Internet site;
» a corporate e-learning/knowledge management solution providing a cost-effective platform for developing skills and sharing knowledge within an organization;
» bespoke delivery – tailored solutions to solve your need.

Why not visit www.expressexec.com and register for free key management briefings, a monthly newsletter and interactive skills checklists. Share your ideas about ExpressExec and your thoughts about business today.

Please contact elound@wiley-capstone.co.uk for more information.

Introduction to Intellectual Capital

What is the significance of intellectual capital in the changing world economy? Chapter 1 considers the emerging role of intellectual capital for organizations:

» the changing equation of wealth;
» why intellectual capital is important.

"Because knowledge has become the single most important factor of production, managing intellectual assets has become the single most important task of business."

Thomas A. Stewart, member of the Fortune Board of Editors

THE CHANGING EQUATION OF WEALTH

Wealth traditionally has been seen as an organization's physical and financial resources. However, over the past several decades that value equation has been turned on its head. Radical changes brought about by revolutions in technology, globalization, and communications have forced us to rethink how wealth in our enterprises is really generated, how best to structure them to be wealth-creating entities, and how to operate successfully in this new era.

The basis for this rethinking is that wealth has shifted from being derived from tangible items to being derived from intangibles. We can see this change by comparing the shift from using a typewriter to using a computer. For a typewriter, the greatest value was its physical value. A good typewriter was a sturdy, heavy piece of equipment that took its value from a long life and efficient design. However, for today's computer, the least important part of its value is in its hardware. By far the greatest part of its value comes from the knowledge, information in the form of databases, etc., and software we put inside it, coupled with our ability to put that knowledge and data to use for our own needs and for those that are linked with us on our networks. In our knowledge-based era, value is directly linked to the intelligence, the speed, and the agility that comes from the processing and linking capabilities provided by the computer. The computer's value is a transformative value. What is critical to see is that this value is dependent upon people, organization, and a host of other intangibles that are rarely listed on the balance sheet.

Extend that notion to an organization. With the globalization of capital markets, financial resources are more instantly available and in greater amounts than ever before. In addition, dominance in tangible or physical resources no longer means dominance in markets. Companies with large inventories and extensive physical plant may be at a distinct disadvantage because of the burden of high maintenance and restocking costs. A firm using a lean production approach can spend its money to get better returns on it in many other ways.

In fact, as financial and physical capital have become commodities, the intangibles of organizations have emerged as the new factor of production that is an organization's ever-greater differentiator and source of value.

In this era where speed, connectivity, and global reach are the basis for competitive advantage, we have a powerful need to understand what makes up our intellectual capital and how to manage it. The intangibles have become the new currency for the knowledge era. They are compatible with the other currencies but have emerged as the differentiating drivers for organizations. Because of their mounting importance and their unique nature, the key to success lies in understanding that we cannot manage intangibles as we have traditionally managed tangible resources.

WHY INTELLECTUAL CAPITAL IS IMPORTANT

Intellectual capital figures in two ways: one way is how we account for intangible wealth in our organizations and society, the other is how we manage these intangible resources.

An understanding of intellectual capital provides a framework for seeing how an organization's intangible, non-financial resources can be cultivated and exploited, in conjunction with the traditional physical and financial resources, to better achieve its desired goals and enable it to navigate successfully in rapidly changing times. Knowledge has become an ever-greater ingredient in a firm's goods and services. It is increasingly embedded in the way we do things and in our equipment. The computers in automobiles are more powerful than the ones on the desks at offices. Intangibles are also major inputs in physical commodities. The physical part of producing information-rich hybrid corn is much less than it used to be (the intellectual capital invested in the corn is the genetic engineering and technology that enables the corn to be pest resistant, tastier, more nutritious, longer lasting in storage, needing less fertilizer, able to thrive in a broader range of conditions, etc.), and oil is routinely discovered and extracted at previously inaccessible ocean depths. In an era where terms like the ''New Economy'' have come to the forefront, there is a need to grasp what the new resources and relationships are and how they can be mobilized for successful results.

While knowledge and intellectual capital have always existed, the rise of technologies such as the Internet, the shifting to networked organizations, and the emergence of a global society all require new ways of thinking about the unprecedented opportunities and challenges we encounter. The world has gotten too complex for the still dominant mode of "command and control" and top-down bureaucratic model to be effective, or even workable. New conditions call for being able to respond rapidly, to be guided by values, and to become knowledge-based extended enterprises. The need for this shift became ever more pronounced over the last decade and no doubt will accelerate even more quickly over the next ten years.

How prepared are organizations and the people that work with them? A number of enterprises have been successful at particular aspects of becoming knowledge-based organizations, but very, very few have succeeded in marshaling the human, technological, and relationship resources to recreate themselves for the new era. Even newly founded "greenfield" organizations rarely have made the effort to establish the infrastructure to become knowledge enterprises. Much of this is due to the fact that the fields of knowledge management and intellectual capital are so new to the thinking of most people. However, as the costs of the old ways become more obvious and the ability to innovate and rapidly respond separates knowledge-based enterprises from their competitors, the winning advantage will go to those organizations that are clearly better able to nurture, capture, share, and leverage their intellectual capital.

Definition of Terms: What is Intellectual Capital?

The most important definition of intellectual capital is the one that makes the most sense for a particular organization. Chapter 2 examines how different definitions came about and how a good definition will lead to a framework for action:

» user-based definitions;
» beyond "goodwill";
» an evolving notion;
» from definition to framework for managing;
» intellectual capital and knowledge management.

"The new source of wealth is not material, it is information, knowledge applied to work to create value."

Walter Wriston, former chairman of Citibank

USER-BASED DEFINITIONS

People from a range of backgrounds have, over time, developed the discipline of intellectual capital. Because each was dealing with a specific set of issues and problems, their definitions directly reflect their unique perspectives and the very specific sets of problems they were working to resolve. Each of the perspectives they developed is true for its specific user need. Thinking that only one of these definitions is correct and therefore the others are wrong is not accurate or effective. A great deal can be gained by looking at intellectual capital through these different definitions. Each lens gives us an opportunity to see our organizations differently enough to derive greater value than any single definition could provide. All of them are valid and it is up to the user to select the definition that works best to meet any particular set of needs.

A definition of intellectual capital from a managerial perspective is:

the knowledge, applied experience, organizational technology, relationships, and professional skills that provide for a competitive edge in the market.

This is a definition that takes into account the people who make up the organization, the structural dimensions of the organization, and all of the relationships of the organization. Definitions that come from a human resource and organizational development background emphasize that the intangible resources are based on implicit human experiences that must be actively turned into the stuff that provides a competitive advantage for the organization.

A more dynamic version of this definition says that intellectual capital is:

knowledge that can be converted into value or profit. It is the value embedded in the ideas embodied in people, processes, and customers/stakeholders.

Definitions from an accounting and capital markets background see knowledge and related capabilities as assets that can be managed as such. That these assets exist and are not adequately recognized is an enormous concern for any valuation of an enterprise.

A definition that is located more in an information technology framework is that intellectual capital is:

> the intellectual material that has been formalized, captured, and leveraged to produce a higher-valued asset.

This definition assumes that knowledge resources can be captured and processed and that the outcomes from these efforts can exist separately from the people that created them.

A fourth perspective is even more active and states that intellectual capital is:

> the ability to transform knowledge and intangible assets into wealth-creating resources.

All of these definitions start with a knowledge base, and are tied to a mechanism by which we transform that capability into a competitive organizational advantage or into profit itself.

All of these definitions are usable and complementary. They all acknowledge that there are intangible resources that are a vital component of the value in an organization and that those resources must be recognized and mobilized for the benefit of the organization. This is true whether that organization is a for-profit enterprise, a not-for-profit entity, or a public sector institution.

BEYOND "GOODWILL"

Furthermore, all of these definitions are true and are much better than the previous catch-all definition of "goodwill" that lumped together all the dimensions of intangibles with the view that says they are collectively:

> an intangible, saleable asset arising from the reputation of a business unit and its relationships with its customers, as distinct from its stock, etc.

While the term "goodwill" contains many of the aspects of intellectual capital, it has serious drawbacks. The most significant is that in our increasingly knowledge-based era intangibles are becoming the dominant value of the organization, which raises the question of whether the traditional accounting framework is worth its salt either for valuation or for navigating the organization. "Goodwill" is based on an industrial-age business model, when intangibles held considerably less value. Additionally, goodwill is treated as an asset with a limited life and so can be amortized. The thing with intangibles is that they can have renewable value. The knowledge that goes into a piece of software can be used innumerable times without any loss of its value, and perhaps with a gain. Brands or patented knowledge also does not necessarily decline in worth over time.

In a related way, the term "goodwill" is neutral or passive. It does not actively reflect that the various intangibles can be discretely treated, and leveraged or managed for what they have become, i.e. the most valuable elements of the organization.

To accommodate the transition into the new economic reality, both the US Financial Accounting Standards Board (FASB) and the Accountancy Standards Board of the UK (ASB) are reviewing the goodwill issue and plan to write new guidelines for reporting on its value. FASB is preparing two FASB guidelines on "Business Combinations" and "Goodwill and Intangible Assets" which will require American companies to periodically determine the fair market value of their intellectual property. Revising the practices and standards concerning goodwill is not easy. There are many controversial and costly reporting issues involved. Regardless of the difficulties, the accounting profession has come to realize that this change must be made. As these standards are accepted and become operational, they will be a major force in moving intellectual capital from being an interesting but relatively minor concern to being a major financial reporting and strategic consideration.

AN EVOLVING NOTION

Intellectual capital is an evolving notion. The more practice people have gotten under their belts the more they have been able to integrate the different understandings that come from its different origins. In the simplest sense, intellectual capital is an organization's wealth that goes beyond what its cash or property, traditionally the two core elements of what is considered capital, can account for. A number of people prefer to use the term intangibles instead of intellectual capital, since these assets are not weighable, touchable, nor do they have dimension. Yet these "intangibles" do have value and can be considered assets, if law and accounting practices permit. Some countries are significantly friendlier to viewing intangibles as assets than others. Australian accounting rules, for example, permit the incorporation of intangible assets in annual reports, whereas acknowledgment of value for reporting purposes is far more restricted in the United States.

The movement to consider patents as assets instead of costs is part of this evolutionary argument. Under current accounting rules a patent only becomes an asset at the transaction point where it is sold. The implications on the valuation of an organization and how it looks at its research and development are strongly affected by the accepted definitions of accounting practices. These patents and other intellectual property will be far more likely to be undervalued, undermanaged, and unexploited unless they are seen as working assets. If this is the case for the most commonly accepted form of intellectual capital then the chances of the other forms of intangibles or intellectual capital never being acknowledged as having value, being appropriately managed, and being adequately valued are extremely high.

While intangibles is a useful term, there is a tendency for intangibles to be considered more from the perspective of assets than from the equally important view of seeing them as capabilities. The narrower view can limit understanding of how intellectual assets work as the basis and ingredients for creating real organizational wealth. From this perspective the broader term intellectual capital may be of greater value for managers.

Even so, there is room for disagreement as to whether intellectual capital is the best term for an organization's non-financial and non-physical resources. One leading practitioner, Hubert Saint-Onge of Clarica Insurance, has decided to use the term "knowledge capital" instead of intellectual capital based on his experience that knowledge capital is more broadly acceptable to the staff of his organization. He sees that most people in his company more readily accept that they have knowledge and that knowledge has value than if what they know and use is called "intellectual capital." The reality is that there is room for different terms as long as there is a legitimate understanding of what those terms mean and how they are to be used.

FROM DEFINITION TO FRAMEWORK FOR MANAGING

Intellectual capital is not only a definition; it is also an operating framework for organizing resources. Intellectual capital has three basic inputs that dynamically interact:

» human capital;
» structural capital; and
» relational capital or customer capital.

These three intangible dimensions are the critical drivers for creating wealth or value. For these three areas of capital to have true value they must ultimately come together to yield "financial capital."

Human capital is sum of all of an individual's capabilities. It is the cumulative knowledge, skill, and experience of the organization's employees and managers.

Structural capital is the embodiment, empowerment, and supportive infrastructure of human capital. It is also the organizational capacity, including the physical systems used to transmit and store intellectual material.

Structural capital is the product of a company's organizational capital, innovation capital, and process capital.

» Organizational capital is an enterprise's investment in its systems, its operational philosophy, and its supplier and distribution channels. It is the systematized, packaged, and codified competencies of the organization as well as the systems for leveraging that capability.
» Innovation capital is the capability to renew the organization as well as the outcomes of innovation. Those outcomes include protected commercial rights, intellectual property, and intellectual assets. Intellectual property is the best-known element of intellectual capital and is the sphere of patents, trademarks, copyrights, and trade secrets.

Intellectual assets are the arena of diverse yet critically valuable resources such as the organizational brand and the theory of the business.

» Process capital is all the processes of an organization that enable goods and services to be created and delivered to internal and external customers. Unfortunately, in most cases these processes are never valued at all. However, when a process is effective in producing value it has a positive value to a company. When a process is ineffective at producing value it will have a negative value.

Customer capital or relational capital consists of all of the market channels, and customer and supplier relationships, as well as an understanding of governmental and industry association impacts. Organizational managers need to come to recognize that they do not need to operate as a self-sufficient island, but instead they can tap into a wealth of knowledge from their network of clients and suppliers to more effectively achieve the goals of their enterprises. Clients and suppliers can test products, give continuous feedback on organizational practices, suggest new ideas and perspectives to explore, co-create new products and services, refer new clients, and operate as sensors for developments in the field and actions of competitors.

INTELLECTUAL CAPITAL AND KNOWLEDGE MANAGEMENT

Intellectual capital can be seen as the framework for intangible resources in an organization as well as a way to understand the stock of those resources. It is a strategic perspective. Knowledge management leverages intellectual capital through an integrated approach to create, share, and apply knowledge for desired outcomes. In that sense, both intellectual capital and knowledge management are two branches of the same tree.

Contemporary knowledge management comes from an information management and technology background and intellectual capital has arisen from an understanding that intangible resources are the hidden resources that add strategic value to an organization. Both deal with knowledge as a prime resource of the enterprise. Intellectual capital provides the structure and knowledge management the means for productively using that knowledge.

Over the last decade, the origins of each discipline have become less significant than the fact that both need to exist and work closely together to effectively maximize the performance and value of an organization.

LEARNING POINTS

» Define intellectual capital in a form that best serves the interests of your organization.
» Common characteristics of intellectual capital:
  » knowledge
  » applied experience
  » organizational technology
  » relationships
  » skills.
» Intellectual capital is knowledge that can be converted into value or profit.
» Intellectual capital is also the ability to transform knowledge and intangible assets into wealth creating resources.
» Major elements of intellectual capital:
  » human capital
  » structural capital
  » customer or relational capital.
» Intellectual capital is the stock, knowledge management is the flow.

The Evolution of
Intellectual Capital

Intellectual capital has existed since the beginning of time, but its modern version is much broader than ever before. Chapter 3 traces how this evolution has taken shape and what its implications are:

» since the beginning . . . ;
» setting the stage;
» value creation and value extraction;
» beyond the firm;
» next steps.

"Companies that make their profits by converting their knowledge into value are called knowledge companies."
Patrick H. Sullivan, intellectual capital consultant with ICMG and pioneer in value extraction

SINCE THE BEGINNING...

Intellectual capital has existed in one form or another from the beginning of human history. Our cave-dwelling ancestors created and mobilized their skills, knowledge, and values for advantage. Evidence of this is the markings they put on cave walls to indicate the migratory patterns of the game they hunted. These caves were also the sites for the rituals that brought new and updated knowledge, skills, and values together, cultivating and sharing them across the generations. The ability to grow and leverage that knowledge made the difference between our Cro-Magnon hunter forebears who flourished successfully and their Neanderthal neighbors who did not have these capabilities and did not survive.

In traditional societies key knowledge was held as proprietary by the ruling hierarchy. It was often guarded and sacred. The priests of ancient Egypt developed a system for knowing when and to what extent the River Nile would flood. It was through their intellectual capital that they could manage the growth of agriculture, which was the basis for the physical wealth of the pharaoh.

The pattern of closely held knowledge and know-how held over the centuries. Maps and trade route knowledge were kept as state secrets. The ability to cultivate and manage this kind of intellectual capital was the basis for states, like Venice, to become the leading trading and military powers during the Renaissance era. In the late 1400s the small kingdom of Portugal, shut out of the rich Mediterranean Sea commerce, catapulted itself into becoming the leading and wealthiest power of its time by strategically gathering, creating, and using its new knowledge in seamanship, ship design, cartography, navigation, and networked intelligence to establish the first global empire. Portugal became a model of what a country could do when it learned how to leverage its intellectual capital.

In the nineteenth century the merchant bankers of Europe, starting as itinerant traders, grew into the owners of financial institutions that financed the wars and empires of the world for over a century. They were able to do this because they knew how to leverage their intellectual capital throughout their global networks. They responded rapidly to changing conditions, cultivating the best information and strong relationships. Their business ethic was so trusted that it became more powerful than the currency they traded. The integrity of their ethic was infused into everything they did and was at the core of all of their transactions. Their fortunes lived and died on trust. The principals of a banking house could trust each other and their clients trusted them, and so they could amass and transfer large quantities of resources globally with ease, providing their customers with the resources they needed.

SETTING THE STAGE

Since the 1980s the creators of the intellectual capital discipline have grappled with the significance of growing value of intangibles in organizations, in proportion to the traditional factors of production, financial capital and tangible resources. This growing gap in value could no longer be easily ignored. They tried to answer the question as to why organizations with basically the same financial, physical, and labor resources could produce quite different levels of value. They assumed that there had to be some other factor that explained the levels of productivity and the market value.

As the information age dawned, these gaps grew far more pronounced as new companies with very little financial and physical resources began to have market capitalization value at much greater levels than other organizations that were heavily invested in equipment, had vast workforces, and sizeable financial capital reserves. All of the buildings, desks, computers, and even cash reserves of companies like Microsoft accounted for only a small fraction of market value and did not explain the discrepancy between the book value of organizations and their market value. This raised major issues about, firstly, how to determine valuations for these organizations, and secondly, how to manage these changing organizations in our rapidly changing times.

These discrepancies were rooted in the radical shift of what determines value and the specific drivers for value in organizations.

Several pathways have been developed to produce what we know today as intellectual capital. One was staked out by Hiroyuki Itami, who published the book *Mobilizing Invisible Assets* in 1980 in Japan, based on his studies of the effect of invisible assets of Japanese corporations.

In 1986, David Teece of the University of California at Berkeley wrote a major paper on commercialization of technology, which emphasized key points of a resource-based view of organizations. This view emphasizes that firms have "differentiated, or unique resources, capabilities and endowments."[1] These resources are "sticky," meaning that they are not easily added or discarded, and are an organization's intellectual resources. In this perspective "skills acquisition, managing their knowledge and know-how and learning become fundamental strategic issues."[2]

Also, during the 1980s Karl Eric Sveiby, in Sweden, started to realize, as he worked to develop his own service-based non-manufacturing enterprise, that this type of organization had very little in the way of tangible assets. He discovered that the one thing that did count was its "invisible knowledge-based assets."[3] Sveiby saw that people in service businesses paid far less attention to financial information and were more concerned about "their people, their networks and their image."[4] Sveiby pioneered the issue of managing intangible assets in his first book, *The Know-How Company*, in 1986. In 1988 he published the *New Annual Report* which introduced the idea of "knowledge capital," and in 1989 published *The Invisible Balance Sheet*. These initiatives paved the way for the idea that knowledge capital was of value to organizations and could be represented in real and convincing ways.

Sveiby carried the idea of working from a knowledge perspective further in his 1997 book, *The New Organizational Wealth*, where he held that managers have to free themselves from the mental straightjackets of the industrial age and cultivate the unlimited resources coming from the ability of people to create knowledge. He stated that, in contrast with conventional assets, knowledge grows when it is shared.

It was becoming evident that useful knowledge was the real difference that people contribute to their organizations and that those contributions show up in all areas: in research and development functions, managerial functions, marketing and sales, and in operations. In short, all areas of an organization were engaged in creating and infusing value in an organization.

VALUE CREATION AND VALUE EXTRACTION

These efforts have resulted in two general dimensions of intellectual capital. The practitioners involved in an organizational development perspective have tended to emphasize the capabilities for wealth generation or the "value creation" side and those involved in accounting for that wealth have tended to concentrate on what is required on the "value extraction" side of intellectual assets. Both are necessary in a successful organization. Realizing the source of wealth generation is the key to continual renewal of firms and having a reliable way to value and market the fruits of intellectual capital is increasingly necessary for an organization to optimize its value to its stakeholders.

The efforts of the 1980s laid the groundwork for journalists, academicians, and practitioners to better name the shifts they were experiencing.

Thomas Stewart, of *Fortune* magazine, began to notice that the traditional sources of wealth of land, labor, and capital were giving way to "intellectual capital." He saw more and more that muscle power, machine power, and energy power were steadily being replaced by brainpower. Intrigued by the notion, he wrote an article called "Brainpower" in 1991. That article was the catalyst for the Swedish insurance company, Skandia, to decide to recast itself as a firm that would distinguish itself by managing its intellectual capital.

A second cover story called "Intellectual Capital" was published in *Fortune* in 1994 and drew an enormous response. For Stewart, the Age of intellectual capital had arrived. He published *Intellectual Capital: The New Wealth of Organizations* in 1997, which aimed to show "how the untapped, unmapped knowledge of an organization" was a major competitive force.[5]

The groundswell had begun. A related major event occurred in 1994 when a group from industry, academia, and policy research met in California to tackle the questions of: *Does the existing management language value knowledge as an essential resource for creating value and wealth? What are the meaningful predictors of a company's future prosperity? How shall we value and measure intellectual capital?*[6] This group became known as The Gathering, and continues to have ongoing sessions focused on sharing experience in developing and applying practices that yield practical results for their organizations.

Leif Edvinsson had become the world's first person to hold the title of corporate director of intellectual capital for Skandia, the largest insurance and financial services firm in Scandinavia, in 1991. He was charged with developing a unit of Skandia with the first-ever organizational structure for presenting the human, structural, and other components of intellectual capital. Edvinsson's team developed the Skandia IC model aimed at creating sustainable performance-based value by targeting four distinct areas of focus (Financial, Customer, Process, and Renewal and Development) along with the one common crosscutting Human area. Skandia integrated these five factors in a dynamic reporting model, which it called the Navigator. This, according to Skandia's then CEO, Bjorn Wolrath, enabled Skandia to have:

> ... broadened, balanced, type of accounting and reporting results in a more systematic description of the company's ability and potential to transform intellectual capital into financial capital.[7]

Skandia drew on its Navigator when it published its landmark *Intellectual Capital Annual Report* in 1995.

Others companies began their major efforts to map and harvest their intellectual capital assets. Dow Chemical created a position of Director of Intellectual Assets and embarked on a major re-evaluation of its research and development efforts and patent inventory, creating the tools and technology to optimize a strategic "knowledge for value" perspective. Hughes Aircraft set up an intellectual capital program called the Knowledge Highway. The Canadian Imperial Bank of Commerce (CIBC) formed its leadership development program grounded on the premises of intellectual capital. CIBC used its growing bank of skills to start a loan program to finance knowledge-based companies using intellectual capital valuations as the key criteria.

In 1996 another foundation block in the history of intellectual capital occurred when the United States Security and Exchange Commission (SEC) held a symposium on intellectual capital. Commissioner Stephen M. H. Wallman convened this session to explore how to account for and report intellectual capital. A result of the session was that Wallman "advised companies to begin experimenting with the disclosure of hidden assets through published supplements."[8]

Shortly thereafter, Dr Baruch Lev founded the Intangibles Research Project at New York University's Stern School of Business. The project has been a center for research into the dynamics of intangible assets and has sponsored four annual conferences, with delegates from around the world presenting and discussing research and trends in the field.

BEYOND THE FIRM

Experimentation in intellectual capital management has gone significantly beyond the firm. Entire countries, with Denmark in the lead, have come to see that they must become knowledge societies, with their competitive advantage coming from the growth of their intellectual capital. Denmark has sponsored a multiyear, multistage effort with a diverse group of companies participating in an experiment to develop an intellectual capital framework that could be flexible enough to account for all of their differences and yet present meaningful insights on how the intellectual capital of these firms is being managed and cultivated.

In the United States, the Brookings Institution carried out a study entitled *Hidden Wealth*.

With every major accounting body in North American, Europe, and Australia involved, the movement to determine the "correct" balance in disclosure and reporting on non-financial value grows. As Edmund Jenkins of the US Financial Accounting Standards Board (FASB) put it:

> "The economy of 2001 is fundamentally different from the economy of 1950 and before. Secondly traditional financial statements do not capture – and may not be able to capture – the value drivers that dominate the new economy."[9]

NEXT STEPS

A convergence of factors is taking place that is making the understanding and management of intellectual capital a working reality for organizations.

» Thought leaders and practitioners are developing the next generation of intellectual capital management approaches.
» There is a gradual acceptance of the legitimacy of intangibles on balance sheets.
» More sophisticated research and tools exist to extract that value.
» There is a continuing shift to a knowledge-based economy.

Learning that managing intellectual capital or intangibles is different than managing tangible assets is a large part of being successful, and that is what is happening in the firms that have taken on an intellectual capital perspective.

Through practice and continuing learning, companies have deepened and broadened their intellectual capital initiatives. In some companies, as initiatives began to yield results, often specific financial payoffs, the limited experiments became learning points that are the seeds for extending intellectual capital initiatives across different parts of the enterprise. Other companies that started out with broader, more visionary efforts have become more pragmatic in their approach and are working to have the intellectual capital efforts reach into the day-to-day activities of their basic processes.

Companies are beginning to realize the extent and types of intangible wealth they have, where that wealth comes from, and how they can leverage that wealth for effect, in ways they never thought about or thought possible.

The first intellectual capital efforts were primarily about either value creation or value wealth. They next generation of initiatives are reaching a new stage where there is enough experience of both perspectives to see the strengths and limits each has and where both can link up to create even greater value for their organizations and stakeholders. The practical base of good theory and practical achievement is building the ground to this new understanding.

MILESTONES

» **1980**: Hiroyuki Itami publishes *Mobilizing Invisible Assets* in Japan.
» **1986**: Karl Erik Sveiby publishes *The Know-How Company* on how to manage intangible assets.
» **1987**: David Teece publishes his paper on extracting value from innovation.

» **1988**: Sveiby publishes *The New Annual Report* introducing "knowledge capital".
» **1989**: Sveiby publishes *The Invisible Balance Sheet.*
» **1990**: Stewart publishes the first "Brainpower" article in *Fortune*.
» **1991**: Skandia names Leif Edvinsson the first-ever corporate director of intellectual capital and organizes its first intellectual capital function.
» **1993**: Hubert Saint-Onge of the Canadian Bank of Industry and Commerce establishes the concept of Customer Capital.
» **1994**: The first meeting of the Mill Valley Group (The Gathering).
» **1994**: Thomas Stewart writes the "Intellectual Capital" cover article for *Fortune*.
» **1995**: The first Skandia public supplemental report on intellectual capital.
» **1996**: The SEC symposium on measuring intellectual capital and intangible assets.
» **1997**: Baruch Lev founds the Intangibles Research Project at NYU.
» **1997**: A number of foundational books are published:
    » Sveiby: *The New Organizational Wealth*.
    » Stewart: *Intellectual Capital*.
    » Edvinsson and Malone: *Intellectual Capital*.
    » Brookings: *Intellectual Capital*.
» **1998**: Patrick Sullivan's book published: *Profiting from Intellectual Capital*.
» **2000**: The Brookings Institution publishes *Unseen Wealth*, the Report of the Brookings Task Force on Understanding Intangible Sources of Value.

LEARNING POINTS

» Cave drawings of animals and migration routes used to educate prehistoric hunters - 30,000 BC.
» Maps, trade route knowledge, and craft know-how were a competitive advantage in the Age of Discovery - 1400 through 1800.
» Merchant bankers operated internationally on access to capital tied to trust - late nineteenth century.

» Knowledge increasingly became a major component of all goods and services – 1970s.
» Core competencies and human capital are recognized as basis for wealth generation – 1980s.
» Articles and books inspire organizations to develop an intellectual capital management capability – 1990s.
» Institutional efforts advocate more transparent and effective standards and protection for intellectual capital in Europe and the United States.

NOTES

1 Sullivan, P.H. (2000) *Value-Driven Intellectual Capital: How to convert Intangible Corporate Assets into Market Value*. Wiley & Sons, New York, pp. 238–44.

2 Sullivan.

3 Sveiby, K.E. (1997) *The New Organizational Wealth: Managing and Measuring Knowledge-Based Assets*. Berrett-Kohler, San Francisco, p. ix.

4 Sveiby, p. x.

5 Stewart, T.A. (1997) *Intellectual Capital: The New Wealth of Organizations*. Doubleday, New York, Preface.

6 Edvinsson, L. and Malone, M. (1997) *Intellectual Capital: Realizing Your Company's True Value By Finding Its Hidden Brainpower*. Harper Business, New York, p. 16.

7 Edvinsson, p. 18.

8 Edvinsson, p. 19.

9 Jenkins, E.L. (2001) Voluntary corporate disclosure in the US. In: 4th Intangibles Conference, pp. 1–2. NYU: Financial Accounting Standards Board.

The E-Dimension

The advent of the Internet created a new and different set of opportunities and challenges involving the development and implementation issues of intellectual capital. Chapter 4 explores what these changes mean to organizations:

» from "atoms" to "bits";
» the new business model;
» from "just-in-case" to "just-in-time";
» people as the owners of intellectual capital;
» case study: Xerox.

"The future arrives at such a pace that physical capital becomes more of a liability than asset. Increasingly, value resides in information and relationships – things you can't see at all and often can't measure."

Stan Davis and Christopher Myer, business writers, futurists, and consultants with Ernst & Young

FROM "ATOMS" TO "BITS"

The e-dimension has brought about a whole new set of opportunities that did not exist before, as well as the chance to reframe much of the basic work of organizations. With the e-shift from "atoms" to "bits" the speed of transactions became instant, location became irrelevant, and intangibles became the currency of exchange. The e-dimension makes the world far more "virtual" than at any previous time in history.

The e-dimension takes everything a step further. Tom Stewart said that the information revolution was about a number of simultaneous and related transformations: globalization, computerization, economic disintermediation, and intangiblization.[1] The e-dimension wraps around all of those transformations and increases the warp speed in which things take place, as well as the options for how events take place. The change is not just technological, but also strategic, touching every aspect of day-to-day activities.

The e-dimension has accelerated the incorporation of knowledge into the design, production, distribution, and use of goods and services. For example, one of the major innovations of the pre-Internet era, the creation of the AMR's American Airlines Sabre reservation system, was an enormous advance in allowing airlines and travel agencies to access travel information and make reservations far more rapidly. In the Internet environment, that access has leapfrogged to anyone who has a computer and an Internet hook-up. The expanded power of information and choice is accessible to anyone who has Internet access anytime, 24 hours a day, 365 days of the year.

The e-dimension has radically reduced the transaction costs for everyone at every point in the production and consumption network. Costs of production decrease because of telecommunications and computer efficiencies and a new flexibility of production mushrooms. This is true both internally in organizations and externally for customers.

It is a transformation that has taken place in virtually every industry. In banking, an investor is able to move money at the push of a button, changing its form from cash to stocks, to bonds, to money markets. The bank, on the other hand, can keep track of all of its markets and determine where its most efficient and effective operations are taking place at virtually the same time.

The same access and managing opportunities are available across all industries.

This is enabled by the change in the make-up of what we transact. The physical nature of goods and services as well as their use has changed forever and has been dematerialized. In fact, there is a convergence of what goods and services are at this point. Companies whose major outputs were physical goods, whether it be computers (e.g. IBM) or tractors (e.g. Caterpillar) are now seeing the real value to customers as the "solution" services they provide.

The previous hard distinctions between goods and services are melting down and the next generation of terms may be coming into play. Goods are becoming "smarter" and being composed of more service capabilities, and services are coming in different forms, and in many cases, knowledge forms. Because of advanced telecommunication links it is now possible for a surgeon in a major health center in one part of the world to demonstrate, and even lead, an operation via the Internet to a field hospital in a remote rural area half a world away. That demonstration can be captured, archived, and recycled repeatedly. In a sense, a lifesaving service that previously was directly available in a limited in-person or video format has now become an unbounded, accessible, digitized set of opportunities. The surgeon's craft now has a global reach at a far lower cost and, potentially, a far larger effect and market. The healthcare institution has a vaster set of services it can offer, and the customers, whether they be healthcare providers or patients, can bring into play far more advanced medical skills and technology at a much faster rate. This is generation of wealth on an unprecedented scale, due to leveraging intellectual capital via the e-dimension of the Internet.

The same explosion of capacities and global access to brainpower and information is true in all areas. Whole new fields have arisen (i.e. e-learning, e-publishing, etc.) but even more importantly, having instantaneous access to strategic and tactical information in a number of formats, plus the ability to disseminate those knowledge resources easily to people anywhere, anytime, represents a wholesale change in ways of doing business.

Not only are information and knowledge becoming available, but the ability on the part of organizations to digest and process these new inputs, and then redesign and reposition themselves, is of great strategic importance. Effectively joining together separate capabilities in technology and in collaboration geometrically enhances rapid learning, work deployment, and effective implementation. That fusion will be the basis for the competitive advantage of one organization or network over its challengers. It is the e-dimension that facilitates this fundamental shift.

Previously, goods and services were mostly composed of a lot of material or labor, held together by a little bit of knowledge, and could have been considered "congealed resources." In the present equation, we are dealing in "congealed knowledge" where the intellectual or knowledge content is at a far higher proportion to the physical inputs.

The e-dimension permits knowledge to be infused far more broadly and speedily, and from more participants than ever before. Whole new dimensions of industries have emerged that are far more robust and less expensive than previous iterations. E-conferencing can bring virtual teams of people together to create, review, change, and finalize designs. The real value increasingly becomes the people who are innovating and operating the processes. The make-up of these teams can easily become much more diverse and multitalented and not just a limited group of people that could most conveniently be brought together due to constraints of travel cost and time.

THE NEW BUSINESS MODEL

A major challenge that organizations face is to rethink their business model in light of their new available e-capabilities. Organizations can stay within their existing business model and primarily focus on becoming more efficient at what they do, repaving the cowpaths to concentrate on cutting costs and saving time, or they can take advantage of their new options to redesign their business model and become "sense and respond" organizations (Table 4.1).

Table 4.1 Transitions to the world of e-business.

	In industrial business	In e-business
	used for:	used for:
Strategy	Prediction	"Anticipation of surprise"
Technology	Convergence	Divergence
Management	Compliance	Self-control
Knowledge	Utilization	Creation and renewal
Assets	Tangibles	Intangibles
Organizations	Structure	Edge of chaos

Source: Malhotra, Y. (2000) "Knowledge management for e-business performance: advancing information strategy to 'Internet time.'" *Information Strategy, The Executive's Journal, 16(4), Summer, 6*

Organizations need to think about coupling the e-business revolution with the business model revolution. Those who can recreate themselves on the cutting edge of responsiveness will have a distinct advantage over their competitors. In a fundamental change, the vastly enhanced capacity to respond rapidly allows organizations to partner their network of customers and suppliers to become organizations of co-creators. This is a development that radically transforms the rules of business.

At its core, this shift is grounded in terms of an organization's capabilities to respond. This is the ability to draw on the past and act in the present while continually sensing and moving towards the future. Organizations need to view their world in terms of the emerging e-environment and revamp their resources in light of the ability to rapidly respond, continuously learn, and grow a set of network relationships.

Security will be not in terms of current assets, but in the ability to respond to ranges of new configurations of conditions. Change is moving at a continually accelerating pace and it is impossible to predict exactly what conditions organizations will be facing in the next week, let alone the next year. It is this anticipation of surprise that must be built into the organizational mindset. Being able to operate at Internet speed, versus bureaucratic speed, needs to become the norm.

For technology, organizations must transition from concentrating on having their intellectual capital embedded in a fixed technology base to an approach that facilitates bringing together diverse knowledge and information and making it broadly and dynamically available across networks.

Management must move to function as resources for, and facilitators of, intellectual capital across their extended enterprises. The complexity of the new environment means they probably know less of the particulars of any situation than the people who report to them. The leaders of the organization need to guide the organization, bring the different parts into conversation, and build the capabilities and values for ongoing responsiveness

In keeping with that, knowledge is not something that is a fixed asset and something to be hoarded. Knowledge is a dynamic, ever-growing, ever-changing resource that must be sensed, cultivated, and brought appropriately into play in every new situation. Organizations need to shift from being activity-based into being knowledge-based, from doing repeatable things to drawing on and renewing a knowledge base that is a community resource.

Part of the new perspective is recognizing the value of intangible resources and developing the capacity to manage them. This is a new set of skills for everyone in any enterprise.

Some measure of structure is needed for any organism to survive and thrive. The question is, what is the right amount of structure for the conditions in which an organization operates? With the emergence of "communities of practice" and new relationships with both suppliers and customers, everything in the organization comes into question. Moving from an internally focused, rigid structure to an extended enterprise network, facilitated by incorporating the e-dimension, will provide significantly more flexibility and necessary responsiveness.

FROM "JUST-IN-CASE" TO "JUST-IN-TIME"

In the past, the range of choice was limited for organizations, employees, and customers. People lived and worked in the same location, and very often were employed by the same organizations for their entire careers. They usually had only a narrow set of life options open to them over the course of their lifetimes. Production and distribution systems were physically-based. Transportation and communications were scarce and expensive resources. Essential resources had to be readily available or stockpiled in case availability was in jeopardy. Inventories of physical resources, such as iron, coal, paper, or wheat were built up "just-in case."

The "just-in-case" model also defined what happened with the workforce as well. Workers were seen as commodities that were brought in, used up, and replaced, just like physical resources. For the most part people were seen as extensions of the physical assets. The skill base for the workforce was not actively cultivated, since the real knowledge for production was seen only to be in the heads of the managers. The workforce was not seen as being able to be entrusted to do more than narrowly defined, specific tasks. During a time of gradual change and limited options, these practices were far more sensible.

In the volatile e-business era, the "command and control" model is an increasingly difficult model to continue to deploy. The level of customer expectations has risen enormously, requiring whole new levels of quality, diversity, and speed of response. The range of choices, both in type and in quality, grew significantly in the 1970s and 1980s, and the emergence of the Internet and World Wide Web in the 1990s ratcheted up the options beyond almost any expectations. Going into the twenty-first century, the range of choices is potentially limitless.

PEOPLE AS THE OWNERS OF INTELLECTUAL CAPITAL

The real revolution is that perhaps for the first time in history, people have control of their intellectual capital resources. They can get up and walk out the door, taking their intellectual capital with them.

As Charles Handy, a leading thinker on business and organization change, put it:

"People now own the means of production in organizations that rely on intellectual capital, on knowledge and skills, because the people have them in their brains, and they can walk out of the organization at any time... It makes no sense to say that the people who own the capital own the people who have the means of production, because you can't own other people either morally or literally, and that is going to change the nature of capitalism.

Secondly, it is going to change the nature of management, because you can't boss people around the same way if they don't like what you are doing. They have a market price and can walk out."[2]

As critical as the e-dimension is, it is operated and leveraged by people. As people discover the power of the e-dimension they can use it to extend and market their talents and intellectual capital. They can either make it available inside the organization or they can use the e-dimension to take the intellectual capital and just as easily send it elsewhere. The Internet has hastened the demise of the old social contract and formed the basis for the necessary links that enable the new social contract.

The e-dimension then is not just a technology. It is the "medium" and the "message," as well. It avails enterprises a basis for a new set of relationships, new ways of doing their business, and a vehicle to reshape themselves, in conjunction with their intellectual capital.

XEROX'S EUREKA!

Xerox's 19,000 service engineers receive more than 25 million customer requests for support annually. Xerox was looking for a better way to train them. After initially going down the road of the traditional approach of a step-by-step logic-based training program, they experimented with a novel way to develop a social fabric that supported knowledge sharing and meaning.

Xerox sent an anthropologist to observe its service engineers in daily work to find out their tacit work practices. The anthropologist followed the service engineers around for six months. He noticed that, as they walked around the copying machines that had problems, the service engineers began to develop a socially constructed narrative. The narrative was not logically driven. In fact, the construction of a narrative was not finished until an understanding of the problem was accomplished. It turned out that the most difficult troubleshooting creates the most interesting stories.

Individual service engineers' tacit knowledge, or know-how coming from their years of experience, was made explicit in their work situations as they shared it with their peers. Xerox developed a community of practice among the service engineers.

Their troubleshooting sessions became their learning zone where they constructed their narratives and co-produced their insights. They then shared their learning through storytelling.

One of the premises was that this was operated as a closed system where management was not allowed to listen in to conversations since trust was a key issue. In their social community, service engineers trusted one another and felt free to share their knowledge. Sharing this experience-based knowledge became part of their professional lives. The social fabric they created in their work supported knowledge sharing and learning.

Xerox recognized the need for the Eureka experiment to go beyond the conventional IT knowledge capture approach, where a classical management information system is set up around the authorized work practices of organizations to support them. In Eureka, Xerox saw that practice structures were emerging within the work of the organization. Rather than formally wire these emerging work practices, Xerox found that its intranet was ideal for supporting informally developing knowledge practice communities.

Over time, practice "tips" were shared over the intranet among service engineers all over the world. These practitioners send in their "tips" to their community of practice, which are peer reviewed and warranted by colleagues. The rated "tips" are then incorporated in the knowledge base which is globally available to colleagues. The service engineers have portable laptops, electronic manuals, and the ability to diagnose problems on a remote basis. Using their knowledge base, they can quickly identify existing solutions or create new ones that can be shared with their community in real time.

Eureka, "ultimately, is an electronic version of war stories told around the water cooler – with the added benefits of a user-friendly search engine, an institutional memory, expert validation, and corporate wide availability."[3]

The knowledge sharing that took place in Eureka had significant business results. Over the two-and-a-half-year period of testing and field deployment, the outcomes were:

» a 300% learning curve improvement;
» a 10% reduction in service time and parts used;
» fewer lengthy or disrupted customer service calls; and
» increased customer satisfaction.

Eureka created a virtuous circle, where social capital was formed simultaneously with the creation of intellectual capital and both were leveraged electronically over the Xerox intranet.

LEARNING POINTS

» The e-dimension wraps around globalization, computerization, economic disintermediation, and intangiblization and moves things to warp speed.
» Costs of production drop radically as the Internet allows knowledge to be distributed and assembled anywhere, at any time, by anyone.
» Distinctions between goods and services diminish as they are infused with electronically enabled knowledge inputs.
» Collaboration plus an effective e-technology infrastructure are necessary ingredients to optimally leverage intellectual capital.
» The e-dimension undermines just-in-case training and replaces it with just-in-time learning.
» People now own the means of production (in their heads) and can easily take their knowledge capital from one organization to another via the Internet.

NOTES

1. Stewart, T.A. (1997) *Intellectual Capital: The New Wealth of Organizations*. Doubleday, New York, p. 7.
2. The Open University (1998) *Intellectual Capital: The New Wealth of Nations*. The Open University, Milton Keynes, UK.
3. Botkin, J. (1999) *Smart Business: How Knowledge Communities Can Revolutionize Your Company*. Free Press, New York, p. 218.

The Global Dimension

The world is going through a new era of globalism which changes the rules of how business operates. Chapter 5 reviews the nature of the new globalism and the implications for the creating, marketing, and protection of intellectual capital around the world:

» the new globalism;
» the death of distance: a 24-hour connected world;
» preparing for the new globalism;
» knowledge: a global product;
» protecting intellectual property in a borderless world;
» changing to confront the global threat;
» case study: Buckman Laboratories.

"The geography of the networked knowledge economy places Germany closer to USA than to France, UK closer to Australia and Hong Kong than Spain."

A New Geography of Trade: Implications of Networked Economy Distances, European Telework Development (ETD)

THE NEW GLOBALISM

According to Thomas Friedman, author of *The Lexus and the Olive Tree*, the current era of globalization began with the fall of the Berlin Wall in 1989. After incubating for about 20 years, the multiple, unstoppable democratizations in finance, technology, and communication came together to bring such pressure on large, immobile institutions and even nations, that the walls of protection no longer held up. The demise of the Berlin Wall was the most obvious, but major corporations such as General Motors, IBM, and even countries like Russia, Brazil, and Malaysia began to experience similar upheavals.

What blew away all the walls were three fundamental changes – changes in how we communicate, how we invest, and how we learn about the world. These changes were born and incubated during the Cold War and achieved a critical mass by the late 1980s, when they finally came together into a whirlwind strong enough to blow down all the walls of the Cold War system and enable the world to come together as a single, integrated, open plain. Today, that plain grows wider, faster, and more open every day, as more walls get blown down and more countries get absorbed. And that's why today there is no more First World, Second World, or Third World. There's now just the Fast World – the world of the wide-open plain – and the Slow World – the world of those who either fall by the wayside or choose to live away from the plain in some artificially walled-off valley of their own, because they find the Fast World to be too fast, too scary, too homogenizing, or too demanding.[1]

With the "democratization of finance," anything and everything became financially tradable. In 1995 David Bowie floated $55mn of bonds secured by revenues from 300 of his recordings. More broadly, in 1999, Reliance Insurance started offering insurance policies on a company's earnings, packaging and managing risk. For example:

"*Times Mirror Newspapers* is in a business of selling advertising and selling newspapers, but at the mercy of a particular variable, the price of newsprint that it does not control at all. Reliance said 'We'll insure you. We'll buy that risk from you and take the volatility out of your earnings, and it will be worth your while on the theory that less volatile earnings are valued more highly by the marketplace. So yes, you'll cost yourself some earnings with an insurance policy but gain market capitalization by reducing your volatility.' ... They made it known they're willing to write much more complex policies in which they take on all of the risks that you don't control because they're in the business of buying, managing, and understanding risks."[2]

The result of this increasingly universal acceptance of risk is that individuals, enterprises, and even countries are more capable of marketing their intangible assets in a global market.

The democratization of technology allowed the average person to participate in this global market with a click of a mouse and an account at a discount broker.

Thirdly, the democratization of information made the knowledge of specialists available anywhere, anytime, to anyone. Information has moved onto the World Wide Web and is becoming instantly available at very little to no cost.

Intellectual capital is future wealth. It is the capacities that are transformed into marketable offerings. Intellectual capital is now not only increasingly the primary ingredient in goods and services, it is also particularly adaptable to the Internet and current global era. It is weightless, non-dimensional wealth that is an instantaneously transmittable, and globally viable, type of resource.

With the availability of the global Internet network, software engineers in India, Poland, and Russia are contracted to provide their intellectual capital to the major IT enterprises throughout the world. Their work may be local but it is instantaneously global in nature.

John Naisbitt has described this as the Global Paradox, where "the larger system [is] in service of the smallest player."[3]

THE DEATH OF DISTANCE: A 24-HOUR CONNECTED WORLD

In the current global era, work on a project can be started by one part of a team in Singapore in the afternoon, continued in Paris in the morning on Paris time with other team members, with feedback coming from New York by the close of business that same day from "community of practice" network members, or even a customer. The threads of knowledge and communication know no boundaries. There is no reason not to capture the opportunity for a truly global, seamless wealth creation process.

Technology, in the form of teleconferencing, allows everyone to be in the room at the same time or to participate asynchronously. Spaces for teleconferencing can be designed so that participants actually experience their colleagues as being on the other side of the same table they are sitting at, even if they are on the other side of the world.

At the same time, e-learning, or distance learning, has broken down time and distance barriers. Monies that were spent on travel and classroom instruction can instead be put to individual laptops, continuous updating of content offerings, and technology infrastructure that a staff person can link to in Japan, Paraguay, or Nairobi with equal ease. The more expensive face-to-face learning can then be targeted to specific strategic sessions that require a much richer set of interactions and relationships. Learning and communication can become frictionless if the relationships are sound and the context for action is robust.

PREPARING FOR THE NEW GLOBALISM

Operating in the new global context requires appropriately preparing for it. The technology may enable communications, but that technology does not determine the quality or effectiveness of the communications. The ease of the network can be deceptive. If there is not a good understanding of the culture and respect for the diversity of values of the members of the network, the grand promise of the new globalism can turn into a quagmire.

Operating in the global environment means that both managers and team members who are bringing their intellectual capital to bear must learn to deal with the social complexity of their far more open workspace.

Robert Johansen and Rob Swigart of the Institute for the Future have seen that misunderstandings based on incorrect assumptions lead to costly, frustrating work situations too often:

"In spite of the growing necessity for cross-cultural co-operation on projects, an increased openness to cultural variables in business, specific approaches to working across cultures are haphazard in most companies. Most companies today provide cross-cultural training only if an employee will be living abroad as part of an assignment. Typically, people working on cross-cultural teams are given no training whatsoever."[4]

Relationships as well as the technology permit knowledge to flow globally.

KNOWLEDGE: A GLOBAL PRODUCT

Knowledge products are a growing share of the total trade in the new global economy. Not only are organizations creating knowledge within their own extended enterprise networks for specific product development, but a sizeable amount of trade consists of knowledge transfer *per se*. According to Mary O'Hara Devereaux and Robert Johansen, "manufacturers are finding that it is more efficient to transfer ideas and have foreign nationals produce the goods and services as close to the local markets as possible."[5]

As knowledge moves across borders, instead of goods and services, it requires that enterprises learn how to manage their intellectual property portfolios, determine what elements of their R&D operations they want to keep where, and understand their entire business processes, so that they can translate them into the multiple cultural environments where they will be deployed.

On the other side of the coin, organizations must learn how best to seek out and accept new learnings as they become available on the global scene. Competition is no longer local. Competition can come from anywhere and any other industry in an increasingly unpredictable fashion. Enterprises need to be aware of opportunities and relationships that will be to their advantage and be able to act on them quickly. The stable, predictable, protected environment no longer exists. Again, being able to be agile, open, and responsive is part of the intellectual capital that must be actively and ongoingly cultivated.

PROTECTING INTELLECTUAL PROPERTY IN A BORDERLESS WORLD

Uncertainty and unpredictability are the enemies in intellectual property. Yet those conditions are embedded in the foundation of the new globalism. As the Brookings Institution Task Force on Intangibles noted:

> "Once an intangible good has been defined by the law as a piece of property, and the rights associated with that property have been delimited, it becomes easier to estimate a value associated with those property rights and to sell, or transfer, or enter into other transactions involving that piece of property ... Anything that increases certainty or clarity in laws that determine the scope, nature and enforceability of intellectual property rights should make it easier to assign a value to the intellectual asset in question."[6]

When patent, copyright, or trademark laws in one country are at variance with similar laws of other countries, the rights of an owner can be compromised and value diminished. The implications of that are that the owner of a piece of intellectual property may be reluctant to license that property or allow knowledge transfers outside the home country. The risk of unauthorized use or piracy may not be worth it.

For some countries, particularly developing countries, there may not be an incentive to protect intellectual property. It may simply not be financially advantageous to pay for patented or copyrighted materials. However, as a country emerges as a significant economy and tries to be a substantial trading partner, disregarding intellectual property rights may come to bring too heavy a price. Companies in countries with advanced technologies may become reluctant to allow their valuable intellectual content to be made available or supported in violating countries. Additionally, inadequate intellectual property protection may be a serious disincentive for investment.

Another strategy in a world where intellectual property is not adequately protected is not to make that material available at all. A number of companies are deciding that instead of patenting, they are keeping their intellectual property as trade secrets.

The Berne Convention on copyrights established minimum standards for signatory nations that provided a great degree of certainty and stability for intellectual property covered by copyright protection. Patents, trademarks, and trade secrets have been significantly more difficult to harmonize across borders. There is a good amount of discussion and the beginnings of a movement to "create an international patent system to extend the territoriality of patent rights in the global marketplace."[7] As the costs of filing and maintaining patents become too great to do business in various countries, the European Union and other regional bodies may become active participants in co-operating to bring such an agreement in place.

As a way to protect trademarks, the Brookings Task Force recommended the development of a centralized international registration system. Currently, anyone, in any jurisdiction, can replicate a trademark or domain name on the Internet, both of which are essential aspects of a brand. The Internet trademark protection system would provide for registration for Internet trademarks and adjudicate all related disputes.

The question is how to reconcile the rights of ownership to patents, trademarks, and copyrights with such a set of volatile conditions.

CHANGING TO CONFRONT THE GLOBAL THREAT

While the new globalism opens the world for trade and individual opportunity, it also has created unprecedented options for international crime and even terrorism. The same Internet that carries the Bloomberg Market Minute also enables instant illegal money transfers, theft of materials that endanger national security, and provides a network for drug consortia and international terrorist groups.

Over the past decade, the United States Federal Bureau of Investigation (FBI) has recognized that crime not only is a domestic problem but has strong international origins as well. The FBI has revamped itself to create a global presence, and also has developed partnering relationships with both the US Central Intelligence Agency and the Department of State. This major change demands the development of the intellectual capital to effectively operate in a far broader landscape. Its human, structural, and relational capital must be mapped and cultivated to meet its new global networking requirements.

While other organizations, public or private, may not have the same type of immediate threats, the actions of the FBI show that every organization must consider renewing itself in light of the new globalism and that its intellectual capital must become a core factor in that renewal process.

BUCKMAN LABORATORIES: LEVERAGING ITS INTELLECTUAL CAPITAL TO COMPETE GLOBALLY

"In my opinion, to compete in the world where change is coming down the pike towards us like a big freight train, we will have to do a much better job of getting the collective minds of this organization effectively engaged on the front line solving of our customers' problems. It is called many names. I call it putting the power on the front line so that we can close the gap better than our competition."

Robert H. "Bob" Buckman, chairman of the executive committee of the board of directors, Buckman Laboratories

Buckman Laboratories is a specialty chemical company that has grown to be a global business operating in over 90 countries, with 500 different products, employing 1300 people, and with annual sales of approximately $300mn.

When Bob Buckman took over the privately held business in 1978, he realized that "we were getting our lunch eaten. We were a multinational organization and needed to be a global organization." He then began his work to shift Buckman Laboratories from being a product-driven company to becoming a customer-driven, knowledge-based company, competing by creating solutions that meet customer needs.

Being a solution-oriented company meant capturing and sharing the best practices within the company. Its conventional research approach to best practices proved to be too costly and slow.

Buckman sought to reshape the company by providing every individual the fullest amount of information as rapidly, effectively, and efficiently as possible. Managers already had much of the best practice information, but that was not routinely shared with the people on the front line who needed the information to deal directly with customers. To remedy that, Buckman developed the first formal system to globally share information in 1987. The goal was to "let the person with the need for the knowledge talk directly with those with the latest and best knowledge, eliminating the confusion resulting from delay after delay."

In 1992 Buckman created the Knowledge Transfer Department (KTD) that was charged to achieve that goal. The KTD built the Buckman Knowledge Network, or K'Netix. The core of K'Netix was a system of forums, where all Buckman sales associates could use the laptops they are issued to post messages, questions, or requests for help.

To support the environment for knowledge sharing, Buckman leadership spent 18 months developing a "Code of Conduct" for the organization. The code, according to Bob Buckman, became the glue that held the company together, providing the basis for respect and trust necessary in a knowledge sharing organization.

The resulting interactive network encourages and enhances collaboration among associates throughout the world, regardless of time or location. For example, a customer in France had a specific problem. An associate in Monaco posted the problem on K'Netix at 4:58 a.m. on a Wednesday. By 2:20 p.m., a US-based associate proposed an answer that had already been discussed and given inputs by other forum members.

In its industry Buckman is a David among a number of Goliaths. Its customers are global and they expect the same level of service in South Africa that they get in Europe or South America. Using the shared intellectual capital of its organization, Buckman has found that it can compete with better knowledge and the capacity for global responsiveness.

LEARNING POINTS

» The new globalism = democratization of:
  » finance;
  » technology;
  » communication.
» Intellectual capital moves freely across boundaries as technology makes geography obsolete.
» Organizations need to accommodate diversity and complexity to access and use their intellectual capital.
» New, knowledge-based competition can emerge from anywhere in the global environment.
» The dark side of globalism is that intellectual capital needs effective international legal protection.

NOTES

1 Friedman, T (2000) *The Lexus and the Olive Tree*. Farrar, Straus and Giroux, Inc., New York. Excerpt taken from the www.lexusandtheolivetree.com Internet Website.

2 Meyer, C. (2000) Presentation at Ernst and Young's Center for Business Innovation *Managing the Future Conference*. Cambridge, MA, October.

3 Naisbett, J. (1994) *Global Paradox*. Avon Books, New York, p. 356.

4 Johansen, R. and Swgart, R. (1994) *Upsizing the Individual in the Downsized Organization, Managing in the Wake of Reengineering, Globalization and Overwhelming Technological Change*. Addison Wesley, Reading, MA, p. 81.

5 Devereaux, M.O'H. and Johansen, R. (1994) *Global Work: Bridging Distance, Culture and Time*. Jossey Bass, San Francisco, p. 29.

6 Blair, M.M. and Wallman, S.M.H. (Task Force Co-Chairs) (2001) *Unseen Wealth: Report of the Brookings Task Force on Intangibles*. Brookings Institution, Washington, DC, p. 73.

7 Blair and Wallman, p. 75.

The State of the Art

As practitioners and thought leaders have had greater experience with intellectual capital, the field has advanced to more sophisticated levels and broader areas of use. Chapter 6 notes the cutting edge developments that are taking place:

» converging threads;
» the environment for change;
» intellectual property;
» changing models of intellectual capital management;
» human capital: the active capital;
» values alignment;
» valuation reporting.

"Commerce is now intermingled with knowledge and information in ways that were unheard of a generation ago. Increasingly, speaking about commercial enterprises means speaking about the creation, the management, the protection, and the application of intellectual capital."

Nicholas Imparato, consultant in intellectual capital, change, and sustainable innovation

CONVERGING THREADS

As practitioners and thought leaders have gained more experience in the fundamental areas of intellectual capital, new ideas, concepts, and crossover themes have emerged. These point the way to dealing more successfully with the basic concerns of the field.

One such concern is developing more effective and comprehensive ways to value intangible resources or organizations supporting better decision-making needs. A second is creating better means to manage the organizational practices to both cultivate and leverage intellectual capital for maximum outcome. A third concern is establishing the overall public policy framework that can acknowledge intellectual capital rights within a territory or country, and worldwide. Related to the first three concerns is forging better models and sets of practices for extracting value from intellectual capital.

The field of intellectual capital is moving toward its next generation. People involved in the specialized efforts of the last two decades have come to realize that they need each other's insights and learnings to create a whole picture. The current leaders in the field are at a point where the founding ideas of the field can be taken to the next level.

THE ENVIRONMENT FOR CHANGE

Certain trends will continue to make intellectual capital increasingly important to organizations. The e-dimension, the need to respond ever more rapidly, and globalization all become part of all organizational and daily life, and companies will have to increasingly infuse intellectual capital into the enterprise structure as well as its goods and services. Those same organizations will also have to find transparent, credible ways to value those intellectual capital inputs.

The challenge is that although the world is moving into the knowledge era, we are still working from formats developed to operate in the industrial era. This is even true for such a new field as intellectual capital. Nonetheless, the emerging transition is causing organizations to shed their industrial-era reference points and create more relevant knowledge-era strategies and practices. The current practices, emerging ideas, and trends that are examined here illustrate this transition.

INTELLECTUAL PROPERTY

Since the 1980s the field of intellectual property has grown substantially. One major trend is that the areas of patent, trademark, and copyright protection have been strengthened considerably through court decisions, legislation, and international agreements. As infringement cases yielded court awards in the $1bn range, intellectual property management began to demand the attention of corporate leadership. On the one hand, companies wanted to be able to better avoid expensive, damaging lawsuits. On the other hand, they also began to realize that their intellectual property had far more value, both internally as well as to other organizations, than they ever thought, and they wanted to capitalize on it.

Leading companies have expanded their perspectives from the starting point of managing their intellectual property and are moving into a much broader consideration of intellectual capital as an enabler of their general business strategy. Intellectual property has come to be seen not only as part of a company's revenue stream, but also as a resource to be used for relationship building, and a substitute for cash in market transactions.

One trend now taking shape is that firms are actively marketing their intellectual property. They are setting up specialized intellectual property marketing components that assess the value potential and seek paying users of selected intellectual assets. In addition, in some cases they are using Web forums as Web bazaars or Web marketplaces where anyone can come and shop. Some examples of Web bazaars are yet2.com, HelloBrain.com, and Knexa.com. In other cases, companies are targeting particular sets of customers who they know would gain substantial value from their specific technologies held in the enterprise portfolio.

Another emerging and controversial dimension of intellectual property is the growing importance of the business methods area. As business methods have become patentable intellectual capital resources, they also need to be assessed and made part of the intellectual property portfolio.

All companies, large and small, will begin to notice that intellectual property does not mean just patents and trademarks. It has to embrace all of the expertise in an enterprise. For example, a company can have skills in handling and facilitating real estate transactions. That is not patentable or something that can come under copyright protection. Yet it is a very important part of that company's intellectual capital. The revolution is in seeing these capabilities as intellectual capital that can be leveraged for competitive advantage and bringing them into the intellectual capital management framework. Management of a firm's intellectual capital should not be a purely local affair, since technologies and other intellectual property developed in one part of an enterprise need to be available to other parts of the organization around the world to yield the greatest value both for internal operations and for external customers.

Perhaps one of the most important trends in intellectual capital is that boards of directors are becoming more aware of the hundreds of millions and billions of dollars of intellectual property and other aspects of intellectual capital latent in organizations. As this awareness grows, they are beginning to hold company leadership accountable for how well they are managing their intellectual property. As a result, intellectual capital managers will be increasingly included at the highest level of senior management as vice presidents or C-level positions reporting to the board because they are core to the entire business.

The increasingly global nature of business is also having its effect on intellectual property management. The costs and time for registering and maintaining intellectual property in different countries can be a sizeable burden. There will be growing pressures to harmonize intellectual patent protection requirements for patents and trademarks, at least between Europe and North America, if not Asia as well. More common standards will allow faster and less expensive processing of applications and counter tendencies to shift to trade secrets as opposed to patent protection.

CHANGING MODELS OF INTELLECTUAL CAPITAL MANAGEMENT

The founders of the modern intellectual capital movement developed their models for how intellectual capital works in the 1980s and early 1990s. The term intellectual capital was created to be a convenient and more readily recognizable name for the intangible resources of organizations. Over time the practitioners have modified the initial notions of how best to name, model, and manage the non-financial and non-physical resources of organizations.

The general model of value creation is illustrated by a set of overlapping spheres of human, structural, and customer (or relational) capital. This model was developed by Hubert Saint-Onge (senior vice-president for strategic capabilities of Clarica Insurance) and it continues to be the most common framework for identifying, creating, and managing intellectual capital resource value, although other models are also emerging. In the spheres model, each circle is a core resource area. The area where the three circles overlap is where value is created. Saint-Onge has been quite effective in using this model as a perspective and a communication vehicle for the service organizations in which he has been involved.

Saint-Onge and others who subscribe to this model work from the premise that it is people, or human capital, that create the knowledge that becomes intellectual capital. Their view is that people are the only active resource and all other resources are passive.

Another view stresses value extraction and has been developed by Patrick Sullivan of the ICM Group and a number of companies, called The Gathering, that have been meeting about issues of extracting value from their organizations' intellectual capital since 1995. Their approach is grounded in the idea that it is the unique competencies of organizations that give them their market advantage. Out of these competencies come an organization's innovations. Value and profits can then be extracted from those innovations. Sullivan and The Gathering have created a model that recognizes human capital, as well as the intellectual assets that are the product of innovation. This model goes further to note that both tangible and intangible resources allow innovations to be leveraged by an organization. The developers of this approach are more involved in manufacturing than service organizations and are primarily concerned with extracting value from intellectual assets such as patents. Nonetheless, they are laying the foundation for the next stage of an approach that actively acknowledges and integrates all relevant types of capital that are involved in turning knowledge into profit.

By including the tangible assets as part of "structural capital," this model has moved towards an integrated approach between intellectual capital and physical and financial capital. This model is an operational framework for the companies involved and they are continually refining it in light of their ongoing experience.

It may have been important for the first proponents of intellectual capital to assert and define it as a separate category when they began to develop the concept. However, intellectual capital has reached a point where it can actively interface with all other types of resources, while still noting its special characteristics and its defining role in twenty-first-century organizations. Sullivan and his colleagues are taking a leading role in that integration.

Daniel Andriessen and Rene Tissen[1] have developed an approach that strives to take into account value creation, value extraction, as well as a systematic view of company value drivers and how all of its resources actively interplay. Their view allows a company to place a measurable value on its intangibles, which in turn give a company a truer picture of its future potential. Their methodology lets a company sort out and measure its value drivers, which lets it see, understand, and unlock the value of its intangibles. Companies are then in a position to make the best strategic decisions and follow-up actions.

Andriessen and Tissen emphasize adopting an economic perspective, in which the economic value is determined by the future value of current output, the new products in the pipeline, and upcoming opportunities. This approach provides a system for calculating the value of company, rather than allowing market forces to decide.

Andriessen and Tissen seek to build on an organization's core competencies that pass the test of contributing to customer value, offer a competitive differentiation, and open a gateway to the future. A company identifies its competencies and breaks those competencies down into intangibles that contribute to the success of that competency: 1) skills and tacit knowledge, 2) collective values and norms, 3) technology and explicit knowledge, and 4) primary and management processes. The value of a core competency is calculated using the relationship between the strength of a core competency and the value it adds to the company.

Andriessen and Tissen help bring to the surface the forces at play in an organization. They add a dynamic addressing of how an organization actually operates and how it can take charge to actively renew itself.

These approaches indicate that practitioners and thought leaders of intellectual capital are pushing the envelope to discover the unique and complementary role of intellectual capital in organizations.

HUMAN CAPITAL: THE ACTIVE CAPITAL

"It is time to take the asset metaphor to a new level, to think of workers not as human capital but rather as human capital owners and investors."[2]
Thomas O. Davenport, organizational and human resources consultant at Towers-Perrin

The emergence of the knowledge or "know-how" society has put people in the position of being the owners of their human capital. Since knowledge workers are owners of their own capital they can invest that capital as they wish. They can make choices. As Davenport puts it, "A worker who acts like a human capital investor will place his or her investable capital where it can earn the highest return."

The trends here are that in the knowledge era, people have increasingly become "knowledge workers" with unique knowledge and skill sets. They are not perfectly replaceable. In flatter, more dispersed organizations, they know their customers and have built networks with colleagues for problem solving. They have become "companies-of-one" within their larger companies and they are in a position to negotiate.

The old social contract has been breaking up for the last two decades. During the industrial era, corporations encouraged people to think they would be working for the same organization for their entire career. As conditions became more competitive, corporations no longer saw it was in their benefit to continue as benevolent, vertically integrated enterprises. They needed to be agile, open networks and broadly entrepreneurial. To survive, their employees had to be entrepreneurial as well.

At the same time that companies shed the "jobs for life" social contract, employees began to be better educated, less tolerant of constraining practices, and more open to operating independently and in networks. People who were discharged from large corporations due to downsizing, mergers, and acquisitions began to be contracted back by their former employers to supply the skills and knowledge their former organizations were now lacking. Frequently, they did better financially and enjoyed their new autonomy. Their entrepreneurism also began to be reflected inside organizations as well, and became known as intrapreneurism, which was increasingly well received by management. Flatter, networked organizations had fewer layers of management and were much more successful the more front line workers took initiative and responsibility for their productivity.

Knowledge workers began to demand greater respect from management as being intelligent people who actively create value. They not only had professional and technical expertise, but also acquired degrees of capability to manage money, people, and projects. There has been a growing recognition that all of the forms of capital, except human capital, are passive resources. It takes human capital to mobilize computer networks, operate plants, leverage marketing, and navigate a financial strategy.

The challenge for organizations is to create the new social contract where the new "cord binding people and organizations derives from the loyalty and willingness of each to provide benefits to each other. This relationship assumes mutual benefit, with neither party elevated at the expense of the other."[3] This requires that everyone involved develop new sets of behaviors, structures, and policies to get the maximum gain from the new relationship. The new social contract requires a shift from management to leadership, from control to collaboration, from exploitation to contribution, and from work groups to communities of practice.

To achieve a high investment enterprise, company leaders and knowledge workers are co-creating working environments where working conditions, learning opportunities, and compensation are to everyone's advantage. The gain for the organization is a human capital resource that sees benefit in achieving the organization's goals as common goals and the gain for the knowledge worker is in opportunities for enhancing expertise, experience, and knowledge, in addition to financial rewards. The challenges of being on the leading edge, opportunities for growth, and satisfying workspace and relationships can be more important than compensation. In this environment working is learning and learning is working.

The new social contract also demands that organizations develop appropriate sets of metrics based on performance. Performance now becomes the metric of achievement, effectiveness, and reward. Both the company and the knowledge workers will use these measures to track how well they are doing, guide their actions, and aid in making the best decisions.

VALUES ALIGNMENT

Underpinning the new contract will be the values that enable the organization to reach its goals. Industrial-era organizations have tended to have one set of values for the workforce, another for middle managers, and a third for the senior leaders. This may have been satisfactory in a traditional command-and-control organization, where employees had their specific job and the knowledge people needed for their work only changed gradually. However, in a fluid, dynamic environment where knowledge needs to flow easily and rapidly, clashing values can make collaboration difficult to impossible to take place. Values form an invisible medium that enables communication and related action. When employees are afraid that they will lose their jobs tomorrow, or when they only think of their immediate and often narrow tasks, despite management desires and availability of the latest technology, collaboration and customer intimacy will not be achieved.

Values alignment may seem to be something that is the most difficult thing to grasp, but it may be the most important foundation. Values are part of a company's intellectual capital. Companies such as Caterpillar and Clarica Insurance have actively explored the values embedded in their history and in their workforce. They found key core values that aligned with their mission and strategy and that virtually everyone in their organization was very comfortable in supporting them.

These companies are value-based organizations. Everything they say and do is a reflection of their values. It is their integrity and provides a basis for trust throughout the organization, and with suppliers and customers as well. Common values and trust allow for frictionless knowledge flow, and for a dispersed workforce to act autonomously with minimum oversight. When staff and stakeholders share in these, it is also far easier to accept and engage them in the continual renewal of their organization.

Another aspect of operating in a global environment is that a values-based organization allows for diversity. When a company is operating in 120 countries across five continents, leadership can anticipate finding a great diversity of values. Rather than have a single set of values to which everyone slavishly is expected to adhere, one US-based company is experimenting with how to recognize and integrate the diverse array of European and Asian values it has found in its numerous locations around the world. Learning to work with and align values brings them alive for the global workforce. They become open to the enterprise that supports their values, their intellectual capital is unlocked, and they feel more comfortable engaging the broader resources of their extended enterprise network to respond to customer and corporate issues.

VALUATION REPORTING

The intangibles that make up intellectual capital are harder to measure, manage, and value than tangible assets. Yet, reconciling the existence of intellectual capital wealth with a well-informed, transparent, reliable, and broadly recognized set of standards and practices is one of the major challenges of the new century.

The dilemma, as the Brookings Task Force on Intangibles put it, is:

"As intangible sources of wealth have grown in importance relative to hard assets, the formal reporting systems that have provided critical information to investors for decades are becoming less and less relevant and informative. These systems, designed to capture critical information about the financial health of hard asset-based firms and the flow of resources through them, simply do not tell investors what they need to know about the true sources of wealth in today's economy."[4]

The critical drivers of wealth creation have become weightless. They include brands, technologies, know-how, competencies, cultural values, and leadership. The lack of good information about value drivers in individual firms and the economy overall makes it difficult for managers to make sensible resource allocation decisions. It also misleads strategic business planners, investors, and eventually governmental policy makers. The result can be a significant misallocation of resources, the undermining of financial markets, and greater inefficiency and cost of investment capital.

Studies have been undertaken to better determine how to identify, measure, and account for intangible assets by the Brookings Institution in the US, the European Commission, the Organization of Economic Co-operation and Development (OECD), the Danish government, and the national accounting boards in the US, Canada, Australia, and the UK. This will lead to making their value more transparent, and therefore more reliable. University research is also taking place in the US, Denmark, Austria, and Australia to develop more effective valuation and reporting frameworks and tools for use in both service and manufacturing businesses.

Establishing a more realistic and reliable basis for recognizing and reporting the value of intangibles will allow governments to better redesign tax structures, as well as monetary and fiscal policy. The implications of the shift to an intellectual capital-based society are massive for individuals, organizations, and entire countries. The work of creating the building blocks for developing realistic, reliable practices has begun. The pressures for the acceptance will also grow over the next few years. The result will most likely be a series of experiments around the world that will, in turn, lead to the next generation of value reporting practices.

LEARNING POINTS

Contemporary intellectual capital issues:
» marketing of corporate intellectual property;
» integrating value creation, value extraction, and reporting models of intellectual capital;

> › recognizing the workforce as human capital owners and investors;
> › aligning diverse values in support of global intellectual capital creation and utilization; and
> › greater transparency of the organizational value of intellectual capital.

NOTES

1 Andriessen, D. and Tissen, R. (2000) *Weightless Wealth: Finding the real value in a future of intangible assets*. Financial Times/Prentice Hall, London.

2 Davenport, T.O. (1999) *Human Capital: What It Is and Why People Invest It*. Jossey-Bass, San Francisco, p. 7.

3 Davenport, p. 8.

4 Blair, M.M. and Wallman, S.M.H. (2001) *Unseen Wealth: Report of the Brookings Task Force on Intangibles*. Brookings Institution, Washington, DC, p. 91.

In Practice: Intellectual Capital Success Stories

What makes a company start an intellectual capital program? Chapter 7 explains how Clarica, Dow Chemical and Rockwell International developed significant roles for their intellectual capital in very diverse organizational settings. It includes:

» Clarica;
» Dow Chemical;
» Rockwell International.

"We used to think about economic growth in terms of land, labor and capital. The driving force is clearly intellect and intellect converted into service to create value."

James Bryant Quinn, academic and international consultant

CLARICA: SYSTEMATICALLY CREATING KNOWLEDGE CAPITAL

"What we have been able to achieve here in five years is way beyond what I would have hoped to achieve."

Hubert Saint-Onge, senior vice-president, strategic capabilities,
Clarica

Clarica is a Canadian firm that offers a wide range of life and health insurance, savings and retirement products, and other financial services. It has its roots in the Mutual Life Assurance Company of Canada, founded in 1870. In 1998 a Canadian government act allowed mutual insurance companies to demutualize. Mutual Life took advantage of that change in the law to gain access to more types of capital and to be better able to reform as it wanted. Demutualization set the stage for the major reorganization of the company and its transition to become Clarica, a stock company.

Clarica has 3 million Canadian and 250,000 US customers. In Canada, that is one person in ten, including employees of 10,000 businesses. Clarica has 5000 employees and a dedicated sales force of 3200 financial advisors who are distributed around Canada in their own local communities.

Setting the stage

In early April 1996, Mutual Life needed a new leader to head its human resources program. Its CEO, Robert Astley, knew that a traditional human resources effort did not meet the needs of the company. He wanted something more systems-based and comprehensive in its view, one connected to the reality of the customer and, at the same time, one that would take an entirely new approach to revitalizing and renewing the culture of the organization. Astley wanted to respect Mutual's culture but renew it in keeping with the changing realities of the marketplace and the realities created by the fact that intangible assets would demarcate the competitiveness of the firm.

He discussed these needs with Hubert Saint-Onge, a vanguard creator and practitioner of the intellectual capital approach in organizations. Their discussions mapped out what was important for a knowledge capital framework at Mutual and how it would be helpful to the organization. Saint-Onge became the senior vice-president for strategic capabilities and was given the license he needed to operate to establish the Knowledge Capital program.

According to Saint-Onge:

"All you need from the CEO is permission to operate. They can't do more than that. If they do, it's not a good thing. I have to be the one that is taking the risks . . . being the one working with the folks to sell the ideas, and getting them to engage in these ideas, to "see the point." If the CEO becomes too strong an advocate of this, it loses its own integrity in terms of what needs to happen in the organization. . . Otherwise it is a personal thing, not an organizational thing."

Saint-Onge is quite clear that he considers the managing of the intangible assets of intellectual capital to be very different than managing traditional tangible assets. The key is that intangible assets are renewable, while tangible assets are expended in use. Since intangible assets have become the greatest share of the value of most firms, those assets need to be actively managed in order to optimize a firm's performance in the marketplace.

The stocks that make up intellectual assets are:

» human capital, the individual capabilities of the members of the organization;
» structural capital, the organizational capabilities; and
» customer capital, which involves relationships with customers, and also with suppliers and partners.

All three stocks are connected and grow based on the exchange of knowledge between individuals, the organization, and the customer.

The company's knowledge strategy became geared to develop the capabilities and relationships that create its intangible assets. Its intangible capital asset framework represents the "stocks" of its intangible assets. Its knowledge strategy functions are the electrical current running between these assets to grow all three of the elements of intellectual capital.

First steps

Saint-Onge started work on his new mandate with an in-depth review of the values that shaped the organizational culture in order to align and renew the tacit knowledge of the organization. Through extensive surveys, interviews, and analysis, the review discovered that the core values that resonated throughout the organization were stewardship, partnership, and innovation.

Clarica, the new name of the company, is based on the review of the company's historical values. Clarica's goal is to "bring straight talk to the customer meant to give the customer power and control over their financial destiny." With its brand message, "Clarity through Dialogue," Clarica seeks to build relationships and aspirations with customers so that they can create opportunities to take actions to realize those aspirations.

At the same time Clarica shaped its technologies to build knowledge processes throughout the company that were fully integrated with the way people did their work, fully linking knowledge and learning. Saint-Onge saw that there is no point talking about the exchange of knowledge unless the technological infrastructure is in place. "Just-in-time" knowledge in just enough amounts was brought to people as they did their work so that they could be more effective at what they were doing.

The next step was to build the management processes that support the exchange of explicit knowledge throughout the organization. The aim was to enable teams to self-organize around complex, highly purposed tasks that required the participation of members from different units. A central part of that strategy was Clarica's intranet, which was created as an electronic platform to transform the culture. Its search capabilities allow employees to find anything they require for their work needs.

Clarica has taken the position that there is no distinction between working and learning. To emphasize that there is no longer any such thing as needing free time to learn, Clarica has distributed cards that everyone has on their desks saying "Learning is working and working is learning."

The new social contract

By developing these capabilities, Clarica eliminated almost every vestige of "training" or learning in the classic sense. It helped its associates understand what is important for their learning, how to plan for it, and how to use the resources made available to them in a self-serve, non-course environment. This effort has gradually changed the culture into being an active, dynamic learning space with associates becoming self-learners and knowledge sharers.

Self-learning has much to do with the ability to renew and develop Clarica's capabilities much faster. It enables Clarica to achieve its ultimate goal of building customer relationships, which it sees it can only accomplish by providing superior customer value at every step in the marketplace. Clarica seeks to bring the customer's perspective to each and every activity in order to demonstrate its brand promise and respond effectively to new trends as they emerge.

Key to its transformation to a knowledge organization is the shift from an entitlement culture, characterized by dependence, to a culture based on self-initiative and independence. Saint-Onge's view is that "the traditional employment contract is based on a benign dependence where employees suppress themselves in exchange for 'a promised future.'" By contrast, Clarica's new employment contract is based on individuals bringing forward their commitment to create value in exchange for being given the opportunity to develop their capabilities and see themselves as a "business of one." Clarica believes that individuals have to be in ownership of their performance for the knowledge strategy to have any chance of success.

The knowledge strategy

Clarica's knowledge strategy provides a framework within which it places its new initiatives aimed at leveraging its intangible assets. It gives a context for growing those intangible assets through the exchange of knowledge inside the organization, in partnerships, and with customers. It outlines the processes, tools, and infrastructure for knowledge to flow effectually to accelerate the development of a capability. The knowledge strategy also delineates a phased approach that takes into account the absorption capacity at Clarica.

Everyone at Clarica is a participant in the knowledge strategy in one form or another, although the members of the Knowledge Team of the Strategic Capabilities unit are its core developers. This Knowledge Team is responsible for the shaping of the intranet, facilitating communities of practice, and supporting different business groups in the implementation of knowledge initiatives. A virtual team of information technology professionals became part of the Knowledge Team and make sure that the necessary "socio-technical" dimensions are reconciled for maximum impact.

The power of knowledge

Just as Clarica was focusing significant resources on demutualizing into a stock company, an extraordinary opportunity arose to make a major acquisition when the Canadian operations of MetLife became available. Clarica recognized that a number of other bidders would also be very interested. It knew it would only be successful if it was able to move quickly since the first bidder to complete the due diligence process and indicate a possible price range would probably get to the negotiation stage. It also needed to use the least amount of resources possible because it had committed substantial resources to its demutualization.

Within three weeks Clarica organized 150 people into 16 teams, each targeting a component of the deal. From the beginning, they were linked by a common knowledge database, where they filed findings, identified issues, and raised questions. This allowed every individual on any team to know what was happening with everyone else who was part of the process. Since there was very little time for managerial intervention, team members were the ones that identified issues, found solutions by building on each other's ideas, and then moved to the next concern. Through the teams' efforts the due diligence and business planning processes for the "integration" were completed in record time.

The quality of the preparation work was so good that negotiations were accomplished in a fraction of the expected time. Clarica negotiators found that they often knew more about the business being acquired than their counterparts across the table. The result was that Clarica was able to acquire a company that was 50% of its size at an advantageous price. Focus and teamwork, enabled by the knowledge strategy, provided a decisive advantage in speed and agility. Clarica has since replicated this same approach for other acquisitions and found it was even easier to operate since it could reuse the processes and templates from the earlier acquisitions with equal success.

KEY INSIGHTS

» All you need is the CEO's permission to operate. If the CEO gets too involved it is a personal thing, not an organizational thing.
» All intellectual capital stocks are connected and grow based on the exchange of knowledge between the individuals, the organization, and the customer.
» An effective knowledge strategy is the electrical current that runs between human capital, structural capital, and customer capital assets to grow all three elements of intellectual capital.
» Understand and respect the values that shape the organizational culture in order to align and renew the tacit knowledge of the organization.
» There is no point talking about the exchange of knowledge unless the technological infrastructure is in place.
» The new employment contract is based on individuals bringing forward their commitment to create value in exchange for the opportunity to develop their capabilities, and see themselves as a "business of one."

DOW CHEMICAL: FINDING THE "HOOK"

"Dow's intellectual capital initiatives today are the key to our sustainable competitive advantage. They are absolutely essential. I am finding that when a new business platform is established, the person leading the platform asks for someone to manage their intellectual capital ... because in many cases, starting out – that is all they have."

Sharon Oriel, director of Global Intellectual Asset & Capital Management Technology Center, The Dow Chemical Company

Dow Chemical is one of the world's largest and most diversified chemical companies, with annual sales of $30bn, 50,000 employees, and a yearly investment of $1.1bn in research and development. It has developed and produces 3500 chemical, plastic, and agricultural products for its customers in 168 countries.

Dow is engaged in an aggressive expansion effort, having recently acquired Union Carbide and several other specialty chemical firms. It expects to double its sales to $60bn by the end of the decade, becoming a tightly integrated, value-adding enterprise, leading in the production of both commodity and specialized chemical products.

The beginnings

Since Dow is a science- and technology-based company, it has always had to manage its inventions. The antecedent of Dow's journey into intellectual capital management came in the mid-1950s when Dow created a function called "Inventions Management." What has changed is that Dow has gone from managing inventions, with a heavy emphasis on counting patents created by research and development, to managing/thinking of inventions as intellectual assets which are creating value for the firm, and getting the different business units to take ownership of these intellectual resources. Dow has now reached the stage where it is broadening its intellectual capital management to encompass its people, processes, customers, and external relationships.

In 1989 Fred Corson, the corporate vice-president for R&D and member of the board of directors, decided that Dow needed to actively manage its inventions. Corson started populating the Inventions Management function with people with a more business-driven outlook and skill base. This shifted the management of intellectual assets from a technical perspective to a business perspective. The new unit had to be able to translate the value of intangibles into business terms.

Key external incentives helping to activate the management of intangible assets were firstly the formation of the United States Court of Appeals Central Circuit for enforcing patents and its subsequent multimillion-dollar infringement findings, and secondly, the fact that globally patent fees went up, which itself was a prime money driver for reconsidering the value of patent portfolios. At the same time Dow shifted the costs for obtaining and maintaining patents from being part of corporate overhead, moving it directly to the businesses. That change created the opportunity to make intellectual asset management a significant enterprise-wide business activity at Dow.

The "hook"

While Dow makes it a practice to build on its invention management legacy, the key involved in applying intellectual capital theory is finding what it calls the "hook." Dow has realized that regardless of whether a company is bricks-and-mortar-based or service-based, any intellectual capital effort has to find a way to make intangible assets visible to the corporation. The task is to find out how to show the value of managing the firm's intellectual capital. At Dow, the "hook" was cost savings. The leaders of Dow's intellectual capital program made it clear that how Dow was operating was costing it money and that it was not getting the best returns on its intangible assets. Dow had license agreements in place that had a negative impact because the annual royalty income was less than the patent maintenance costs for the licensed patents. That monetary hook enabled Dow to start applying the theory.

When a new business director took over one of the business units, Sharon Oriel went to him and said "How would you like to save $3mn?" The manager looked at her and said "Is it legal?" She told him "Yes," and he said "Make it happen!" Then he asked "What did I authorize you to do?"

Dow had acquired a group of technologies from Upjohn's chemical division several years earlier. It was clear that it was not going to use some of them. The new manager's predecessor had the attitude that "We will keep them here just in case." The new business manager understood that the business was never going to leverage all the technologies, and understood that there was a cost to keeping them on the shelf. The "hook" was the savings. The manager knew that Oriel had done the homework on the 200 patents and 15 agreements involved. He turned to her and said "Make it happen." That established the basis with that business director to begin managing his intangible asset portfolio.

Because Dow intellectual capital practitioners earned their credibility by providing this type of real value to the business units, the company is now ready to wrestle with a broader intellectual capital effort.

The in-house database

Another important advantage that Dow had in managing its intangibles was that in the 1980s it had started an in-house electronic database containing all its disclosures of inventions, all its filed patents, as well as its issued patents and agreements dealing with intellectual property. Dow can easily identify what assets belong to what business and what products are protected across the entire organization.

We show the money

Dupont Dow Elastomers is an example of the leveraging power of intellectual capital management. Dupont dominated the market on elastomers. It had the necessary manufacturing and the sales structures, but its technology was aging. Dow, on the other hand, had a new technology, but a very small elastomers business. Dow's contribution to the new partnership was its new technology. It brought no bricks and mortar, just its intellectual capital, while Dupont brought its infrastructure. The instant outcome was a billion-dollar company.

Stories like this make an enormous impact at Dow. Using its intellectual capital in major litigation and in creating new sales where its intellectual capital has come to play a prominent role has produced major gains for Dow. Dow's "hook" is simply that intelligent use of its intellectual capital makes a significant money difference. Dow intellectual capital practitioners even have made up T-shirts that say, "**We show the money**."

When a new business unit is established, the person leading that platform asks for someone to manage their intellectual capital, because, in many cases, that is all they have. In that way, Dow's intellectual capital initiatives have become key to sustaining its ongoing competitive advantage.

A community of practice

The intellectual capital management function is facilitated by the Intellectual Capital Tech Center. The role of the Tech Center is to provide a centralized effort to develop and identify better intellectual capital practices and to facilitate the implementation of these better practices in the businesses. The process leaders in the Tech Center partner with the business-aligned IA manager to create value from the intangibles portfolio. They make sure that the portfolios are being managed and know how to effectively use the in-house database. They are a small, co-located group that easily shares knowledge, creates new knowledge, and captures knowledge. They have become the linchpins for both best practices and continuous improvement. Additionally, the Tech Center is responsible for training and educating all of the new managers. They come to understand that intellectual capital management is not a solo, but a team, sport.

Dow has intellectual managers located in Latin America, Europe, and the Pacific. On a global basis, it does not send somebody from the US to impose outside rules, but rather, it brings the intellectual capital managers of a region together to go over the intellectual capital issues that are specific to their locations. The links are simultaneously in the regions as well as with the corporate headquarters in Midland, Michigan.

Today each business unit has at least one intellectual capital manager, with some having as many as five, depending on the size of the intellectual capital portfolio that needs to be managed. The intellectual capital management leaders have an R&D background, with technical competence, but also have developed the complementary business, communication, and human relationship skills needed to be successful in their work. Jobs in intellectual capital management are very desirable and Dow has set them up as a job family, with four levels that encourage career progression.

When a business has a particular need, that business takes the lead on that issue. When the value of that particular intellectual capital effort is demonstrated, word travels to other business units who might see the value and need. Some business units at Dow deal in very old products and emphasize preserving the value of their intellectual capital, while the new businesses may much more emphasize growing their intellectual capital. One size of business strategy does not fit all, but each unit can take on and share learnings and best practices that are applicable to it. Dow has come to understand that the fundamentals of intellectual capital management cross all businesses, despite their differences.

Building towards the future

Dow has succeeded in the shift of emphasis from intellectual property to intellectual capital. Intellectual capital has become part of the Dow lexicon and a talking point for the CEO. Business presidents now talk about their intellectual capital in the same manner that they discuss their plants, customers, etc. Dow's scientists and engineers have come to ask "What is the value of my invention and how will it be used?" Instead of judging people on their sheer numbers of patents, the value proposition is: "What is the value that is being created for Dow?" Further, that value can take shape in a whole myriad of forms, whether it is as a trade secret, through publishing a paper, or by licensing.

Building on its technical achievements, Dow is engaging in managing both its human capital dimension and its business dimension. When a new business platform is established, Dow not only has come to look at market size and competitors, but also what the "intellectual asset lie of the land" is. This is taking its intellectual capital management effort to a whole new level, both globally and in all its business units.

KEY INSIGHTS

» Find the "hook." Recognize what your culture is. Start from what is valuable to your people, build credibility, and grow from there.
» Gain senior management support.
» Develop and use stories of successes to ripple throughout the organization.
» Build an enabling network, not an empire.
» One size does not fit all. Employ a business strategy that acknowledges that each business unit has its own history, products, and services, and will use intellectual capital management to better its own outcomes.
» Recognize the role that intellectual capital has in the many cultures and then create an intellectual capital culture that cuts across those cultures.

» Create linkages throughout the different parts of the organization.
» Design intellectual capital skill-building sessions to also serve as
team-building sessions.

ROCKWELL INTERNATIONAL: THE ROAD TO CHANGE

"The average company on the S&P 500 has some 80% of its
market cap in its intangibles. Boards of Directors are going to
find themselves in a position where they have to demand active
management of their intangibles. How can you ignore them?"

*James P. O'Shaughnessy, vice-president and chief intellectual
property counsel, Rockwell International Company*

A $1bn dilemma

Rockwell International is a company that has gone through substantial
changes over the last decade. It has restructured itself from being a
multibusiness holding company, involved in a half-dozen markets, and
has become an enterprise with one highly focused business. In 1996 it
was making things like the aerospace shuttle and B1 bombers. It has
since sold its aerospace, defense, printing, semiconductor, automotive,
and avionics businesses and is now a 20,000-person enterprise that
fully concentrates on providing the equipment and software for factory
automation.

The modern era for intellectual capital management at Rockwell
International began in 1996. Rockwell realized it needed someone to
devote full-time attention to what had potentially become extremely
costly intellectual property issues. As Rockwell went through a transformation from an aerospace and defense-based enterprise to a commercial
organization, it lost a great deal of protections afforded to aerospace
companies supplying United States Defense Department needs, particularly protections against patent infringement.

Companies operating for or on behalf of the US federal government were insulated from many of the patent concerns commercial
companies have because the US government exempts itself from its

own patent laws. This environment, in which it historically operated, underlay Rockwell's decision-making and low concern over patent infringement.

Rockwell's executive corps had not been trained for navigating in an environment that changed dramatically, which is exactly what happened when its commercial activities shifted to being the predominant side of its business. It took time for Rockwell to catch up with what quickly became extremely costly patent issues, as Rockwell became subject to a large docket of adverse patent litigation that made it potentially liable for $1bn in awards. This new reality demanded both a different level and kind of response than the company was prepared for. Normally it would dip into its different pockets for a $1mn damage award here and there, but $1bn in cash was beyond the capacities of the enterprise.

Bursting the litigation bubble with intellectual capital value

Rockwell's current chairman asked James P. O'Shaughnessy to join the company to manage the bubble of litigation. Rockwell had only just started to appreciate what intellectual property and intellectual capital were and what they meant. Traditionally these concerns were of minor consequence relative to its procurement and production issues. But now the dimensions of the problem were so large that it could not do the usual thing of trying to find ready cash, and cash alone, to solve this set of problems. The company had to find other acceptable values to add to the cash, and in this case it was its intangible assets that came to the rescue. Rockwell began to understand that while cash is important and essential as the lubricant that allows transactions to go forward, because it is a lubricant it can sometimes also be used in much smaller quantities that most people appreciate.

O'Shaughnessy proposed to make a shift from the normal value equation and instead say that value is a function of the combined values of intellectual capital and financial capital. He felt that, while not perfectly substitutable, the two are roughly exchangeable over a fairly significant range. As he put it:

"If I had a $1mn problem to solve, I could probably not just offer up $1mn of intellectual capital... but we can solve $1mn problems with maybe $500,000 of intellectual capital value and $500,000 in cash (financial capital), taking the pressure off the balance sheet by that much. The transaction proceeds because the other party agrees on the valuation. Their gain was $1mn in value. It's just that the composition is somewhat different from where it would be $1mn in cash. . .

"Where the rabbit is in the hat is that it does not cost $500,000 in cash to generate $500,000 in intellectual capital value. Sometimes the value is already there and you just have to scour the company for it. At other times it needs to be created, but we find that we get leverages in excess of 10:1. We can create $500,000 in intellectual capital value for $50,000 or less.

"Since it might cost $500,000 in cash plus $50,000 to generate the other $500,000 in value, I have taken $450,000 in pressure off of the balance sheet.... Further, that $500,000 in intellectual capital may be useful in other settings, and it might be able to be used over and over again, significantly lowering the marginal costs of generating it."

By using an intellectual capital management perspective Rockwell was able to settle over $1bn in litigation using very little cash. Cash requirements came to be less than 10%, and the balance was intellectual capital values that were created, transferred, and put to use productively. The leveraging effect of intellectual capital was demonstrated with great effect through that process.

From negative lessons to positive examples

Resolving the massive patent dilemma served as a valuable lesson in helping Rockwell focus on what is really important to it. It has learned from that negative lesson and moved on to some positive examples.

Rockwell now has a large portfolio of intellectual assets that is broader than just its patents. These mainly technology-based intellectual assets have very substantial but latent value. The problem with latent value, though, is that it takes something proactive to convert the latent value into reality. In response, Rockwell created Rockwell Technologies to transform its latent intellectual assets into a variety of tradable resources by:

» converting the latent value of its intellectual assets into cash;
» using its intellectual assets in transactions;
» using its intellectual assets with alliance partners as inputs into critical components or equipment; and
» making its intellectual assets available to create relationships with clients or suppliers.

To nurture its thinking on how to better manage its intellectual assets, Rockwell became part of a group of what has become 30 companies, called the ICM Gathering, that meets regularly to discuss topics involved in technology commercialization. Rockwell uses a process model developed by Gathering members to frame and stimulate communications, provoke analysis, and validate its decision-making.

Rockwell Technology employs different venues for creating real dollar value for its latent intellectual assets. It works from the perspective that it is the buyer's or seller's "context" that determines value. It is expanding its range of buyers by participating in Internet intangible assets markets, such as yet2.com, where the buyers' "context" determines their bids on available technology packages. Potential buyers may have needs that differ markedly from those the technology was originally created for, yet that technology may be precisely useful for their particular needs, and they may value it even more highly than it was for the purpose for which it was originally intended.

For the real gems of its technology portfolio, Rockwell has a good sense of the value context. It conducts a rigorous review process of the half-dozen or so major technologies within the company that are truly world class. It knows who can use them and it uses its array of analytic tools to price them. After the hard work of identifying the right parties and getting the right data together is done, it is then able to engage in meaningful negotiation and appropriate technology transfer, where it converts latent value into something meaningful – usually, but not always, cash.

Rockwell has intentionally organized to operate an opportunistic, but informed, process. It spends a great deal of time on the preparation side, so that when opportunities arise, it is able to seize them expeditiously. Rockwell is now able to identify these opportunities, whereas in the past it would stumble over them as if nothing happened and continue on.

Committees within Rockwell work with Rockwell Technologies to identify the right technologies to commercialize outside the company. At this stage, Rockwell also understands how to commercialize its own technologies within its own core markets. Its current challenge is to get better at recognizing how to commercialize its technologies in non-core areas where substantial latent value lies.

$V = f(IC + FC) = Outcomes$

Five years ago, Rockwell began with a program designed expressly to solve a massive but limited problem. It has since grown to be able to focus on opportunities that make sure its intellectual capital program supplements and supports the overall business mission and its operating fields. The big change is that Rockwell is paying attention to its intellectual capital and is measuring and managing it.

The breakthrough came when O'Shaughnessy began using the simple equation of $V = f(IC + FC)$. He was able to use that formula to clearly communicate the new flexibility and value that Rockwell would have available to it. That gained attention. Rockwell now knows it can conserve its resources and leverage its intellectual capital in ways that make a significant difference in its bottom line.

KEY INSIGHTS

› A simply-put equation, $V = f(IC + FC)$, got the attention of people in the organization, enabling them to see that intellectual capital was a real resource that could be interchangeable with financial capital to take the pressure off the bottom line.

» Solving a significant organizational problem using intellectual capital can open the door to creating opportunities.

» Intellectual assets have substantial but latent value. That latent value needs to be converted to real, cash value.

» In addition to being a tradable, or cash-generating resource, a significant use of intellectual capital can be to create relationship capital for the enterprise.

» All value is contextual. In an undefined market the buyer will be the one to determine the context for value, but the seller will most likely be in a good position to determine contextual value for its core intellectual assets.

» It may be appropriate to set up a separate business to handle the valuation and marketing of a company's intellectual assets.

» A working model for how intellectual capital supports organizational strategic goals helps stimulate dialog and better decision-making.

» E-business market trading sites offer unprecedented global access to potential paying users of intellectual capital.

» Continuous communication to all parts of an organization is necessary for successful buy-in and participation.

» Knowledge creation and knowledge extraction are both essential for an effective intellectual capital program.

Key Concepts and Thinkers

Intellectual capital has developed its own language and frameworks. Chapter 8 provides an overview of key terms and the leading figures in the field:

» a glossary of intellectual capital;
» key concepts;
» key thinkers.

"We make doors and windows for a room. But it is the spaces that make the room livable. While the tangible has advantages it is the intangible that makes it useful."

Lao Tzo, Chinese philosopher, 600 BC

A GLOSSARY OF INTELLECTUAL CAPITAL

Capitalization - Creating financial value from intangible assets.

Complementary assets - Business assets of a firm used to create value in the commercialization process.

Culture - The combined sum of individual opinions, shared mindsets, values, and norms.

Customer capital - See Key concepts below.

Explicit knowledge - Knowledge that is articulated, codified, formal, systematic, and easily shared and communicated. It is found in the words we speak, in any written commentary, such as product specifications, scientific formulas, or computer programs, as well as in any recorded data.

Future earnings capability - Ability to create and capitalize on intellectual capital.

Human capital - See Key concepts below.

Innovation capital - The capability to renew the organization as well as the outcomes of innovation. Those outcomes include protected commercial rights, intellectual property, and intellectual assets.

Intangibles - Non-physical factors that contribute to or are used in producing goods or providing service, or that are expected to generate future productive benefits for the individuals or firms that control their use (*Unseen Wealth*, p. 10).

Intellectual assets - The codified tangible, or physical, descriptions of specific knowledge to which a company can assert ownership rights. Intellectual assets are diverse yet critically valuable resources that can range from intellectual property to such concepts as the organizational brand and the theory of the business.

Intellectual capital - Knowledge that can be converted into value (for definitions and a full discussion, see Chapter 2).

Intellectual property - Intellectual assets that receive legal protection, usually in the form of patents, copyrights, trade secrets, trademarks, and, in different countries, for special categories.

Knowledge – Meaningful links people make in their minds between information and its application in action in a specific situation.

Multiplicative effect – Leveraging that takes effect in the interaction between human capital and structural capital.

Organizational capital – An enterprise's investment in its systems, its operational philosophy, and its supplier and distribution channels. It is the systematized, packaged, and codified competencies of the organization as well as the systems for leveraging that capability.

Process capital – All of the processes of an organization that enable the creation and delivery of goods and services. When a process is effective in producing value it has a positive value. When a process is ineffective at producing value it will have a negative value.

Relational capital – See Key concepts below.

Structural capital – See Key concepts below.

Tacit knowledge – Knowledge that resides in an individual, often as a skill, an ability, or know-how.

Value creation – The generation of new knowledge and its conversion into innovations with commercial value. Value creation activities include education, knowledge development and sharing, innovation, creation of supporting organization structures, and managing values and culture.

Value extraction – Involves converting the created value into a form that is useful to the organization, whether it is innovations into cash or into some form of strategic position. It usually involves codifying knowledge created by the enterprise's human capital resources to build databases, create valuations, support decisions, establish and enhance capabilities, and convert for commercial purposes.

KEY CONCEPTS

Customer capital

The value of the customer base, customer relationships, and customer potential.

Human capital

All of the individuals' capabilities. It is the cumulative knowledge, skill, and experience of the organization's employees and managers that can be invested to meet the task at hand. Human capital cannot be owned by a company but only by the individuals that work with it. Human capital is involved in work that is a two-way value exchange between the individual and the organization, not a one-way exploitation of an asset by its owner.

An effective knowledge-based enterprise will convert the human capital of its workforce into structural capital, which, in turn, can be repeatedly converted into financial capital. Knowledge-based enterprises motivate their human capital resources to make their knowledge and know-how explicit and codified so that it can be widely shared and internalized into the practices and structure of the organization.

Human capital is the only active capital in an organization and the source of its innovation and conversion to value. All other capital is passive. Moving from a traditional dependency, entitlement culture to one geared to self-initiatives and independence is the hallmark of knowledge organizations. Individuals have ownership of their performance in this new social contract and see themselves as a "business of one." This new model is key for organizations to optimize the human capital resources of the workforce for strategic enterprise outcomes. In this equation, it is the responsibility of the enterprise to provide the context for the individual to grow and develop his or her human capital.

Intellectual capital management

Intellectual capital management is the active management of intellectual capital resources. It has three dimensions: value creation, value extraction, and value reporting. Effective intellectual management makes sure that these three endeavors are balanced to reflect meeting the goals of the organization.

Value creation enables intellectual capital to come into existence so that it can be shared and leveraged. Value extraction brings intellectual capital resources to where they can be converted into some type of value for the enterprise. Value reporting enables an accurate reflection of the value of intellectual capital for both decision-making and analysis by internal management, and externally for shareholders, the capital markets, and other stakeholders.

Intellectual capital value scheme

A model which illustrates the building blocks that collectively form the foundation of the enterprise's intellectual capital and its relationship to market value. In one view (Leif Edvinsson), intellectual capital is broken down into human capital and structural capital, which is then broken down into customer and organizational capital. Organizational capital is composed of both process and innovation capital.

Knowledge-based enterprise

A knowledge-based enterprise embeds knowledge and learning into its products, processes, and services. Knowledge-based enterprises are not solely high technology companies. All organizations are to one extent or another knowledge enterprises. Seventy percent of the value of an ear of corn is the knowledge that went into it. Thirty percent of the value of a barrel of oil is derived from knowledge inputs. Smart products and services actively leverage knowledge to create value. Hardware companies like IBM build their knowledge into their computers, while software companies like Microsoft build their knowledge into their software. It is the degree to which the knowledge is identified and leveraged for outcome that determines the degree to which an organization is a knowledge-based enterprise.

Knowledge recipes

Knowledge recipes are formulas that bring together software (explicit and codified knowledge) with hardware (physical objects used in production) and wetware (tacit knowledge and capabilities) to create value. These recipes can be replicated and shared rapidly throughout an organization or network to produce desired outcomes. There can be knowledge recipes for growing crops, establishing offices in new territories, or learning any skill. The quality and extent of knowledge recipes an organization is developing in its pipeline will determine its capacity to produce wealth over time.

Relational capital

Relational capital is composed of all the external relationships of the organization. This includes all of the market channels, customer and supplier relationships, as well as industry associations and governmental regulatory bodies. As organizations move towards becoming extended enterprises, the relationships in the emerging network will enable the trust and communication necessary for any effective strategy and action. Relationship capital is also essential for an enterprise to co-create its products and services with its customers, as they provide continuous, rapid feedback to the enterprise as to what will satisfy their needs. E-business and related technologies have created tremendous new opportunities to grow and support the management of relationship capital, by establishing extensive relational databases that can provide instant responses to customers, along with extensive customer histories and preferences.

Structural capital

Structural capital is the embodiment, empowerment, and supportive infrastructure of human capital. It provides the environment that encourages individuals to invest their human capital to create and leverage its knowledge. It encompasses the organizational capacity, including the physical systems used to transmit and store intellectual material. It is all of an organization's organizational capital, innovation capital, and process capital.

Intellectual capital by itself is of little value without the leveraging effect of the firm's supporting structural capital resource. In the approach that focuses on intellectual capital extraction, a major component of structural capital also includes what is called complementary business assets. These are the business assets of a firm that are used to create value in the commercialization process, and include manufacturing, distribution, and marketing capabilities.

Value: sources and conversions

An enterprise has two sources of intellectual capital value that it can convert into profits: its innovations, and the business practices and processes that convert those ideas and are applied to those innovations. At the same time, an organization has seven mechanisms available to it that it can use to convert its innovations into cash: direct sales, out-licensing, joint assets, strategic alliances, integration with current business, creating a new business, and donating the innovation, which produces a tax write-off.

To optimize the value of their intellectual capital, companies need to look at the largest numbers of types of combinations for its innovations and practices and determine the best set of conversion mechanisms that will yield an optimal cash or strategic advantage to the enterprise. It can then choose which sets of choice best advance its strategic goals. A company can consider seeking to use an innovation to bolster a strategic alliance in one setting, licensing it in another, and establishing a joint venture in a third market.

KEY THINKERS

Leif Edvinsson

Leif Edvinsson is a key contributor to the theory and practice of intellectual capital. He is the founder and CEO of UNIC (Universal Networking Intellectual Capital AB) whose mission is to generate new insights as to what an organization's intellectual capital is, as well as how to grow, appraise and better understand how to commercialize it. His sees himself serving as a catalyst for the possibilities inherent in the new era of intangible wealth.

Edvinsson was formerly the corporate director of intellectual capital at the Skandia Group, where many of the fundamental ideas of intellectual capital as a whole organizational framework were developed and put into operation. He held the first position of its type in the world of director of intellectual capital at Skandia, AFS in 1991. During his tenure at Skandia, he oversaw the creation of its first Intellectual Capital Annual Report supplement, which outlined how Skandia used this hidden, intangible value for the benefit of customers and shareholders.

He is co-author of a defining work in the field, *Intellectual Capital: Realizing Your Company's True Value by Finding Its Hidden Brainpower*, as well as a contributor to numerous other books and journals. Edvinsson was recognized for his achievements by being given the "Brain of the Year" award from the Brain Trust of the UK in 1998.

Edvinsson views the challenge of intellectual capital leadership as changing its mindset so it can use the structural capital of organizations to turbo-charge the capabilities of human capital, which, in turn, can be transformed into new structural capital. The outcome of this is the development of authentically intelligent organizations, but organizations of a very different nature. These new organizations may well evolve into becoming communities, and, instead of functioning as employees, its participants will become citizens of those communities.

Edvinsson is developing an intellectual capital rating tool for assessing factors supporting a company's ability to increase its competitiveness and better understand the role of intellectual capital in stock market valuations, annual reports, and credit analysis. His work on the intellectual capital multiplier is used to value the springboard effect that the structural capital of company offers to leverage its human talents,

Edvinsson is foremost a visionary of intellectual capital. He says, ''The future is our home.'' A sense of the future underlies the building of a number of Future Centers throughout the world, which are experimental stations to prototype how to create the organizational capital that will be the basis for creating the wealth of the new millennium.

Links

www.unic.net
www.intellectualcapital.se
www.iccommunity.com

Highlights

Books:

» (1997) *Intellectual Capital*, with M. Malone. Harper Business, New York.

Baruch Lev

Baruch Lev is the Philip Bardes Professor of Accounting and Finance at New York University, Stern School of Business, and the Director of the Vincent C. Ross Institute for Accounting Research and the Project for Research on Intangibles. He earned his MBA and PhD degrees from the University of Chicago. He is a permanent visitor at Ecole Nationale Des Ponts and Chaussées (Paris) and City University Business School (London).

Professor Lev began his pioneering research in the field of intangibles in the early 1990s as a colleague of David Teece at UC Berkeley. His work spans three books and over 75 research studies published in the leading accounting, finance, and economic journals. This research concerns the optimal use of information in: investment decisions; business valuation issues; corporate governance; and intangible investments (intellectual capital). In particular, his focus is on measurement, valuation, and reporting issues concerning intangible investments.

Lev lectures internationally and conducts executive seminars on finance, accounting, and intellectual capital issues, working closely with such institutions as the Securities and Exchange Commission, the Financial Accounting Standards Board, the OECD, the European Union, and the Brookings Institution.

Lev has organized annual conferences on intangibles, held at New York University, in New York City, which are significant gatherings in the field for both academics and practitioners.

As Professor Lev put it: "The new accounting has to depart from the old accounting, which is based on costs. While costs will always be important, the new accounting is based on values... The future is based on intangibles. The old accounting is a beautiful system. The virtue of the old system is that it is based on facts. The problem is that these facts are no longer relevant."

Lev is developing a methodology for measuring the value of intangible assets and determining "intangibles-driven" earnings. He has recently completed a report for the Brookings Institution, *Intangibles: Measurement, Management and Reporting*, which explores the nature of intangibles and their reporting, and is available on his Website.

A number of research documents, including "Markets in Intangibles: Patent Licensing" and "New Accounting for a New Economy," are also available on Lev's Website, as well as video interviews, all of which are well worth accessing.

Link

www.stern.nyu.edu/~blev/

Highlights

Book:

» (2000) *Intangibles*. The Brookings Institution, Washington, DC.

Articles:

» (1999) "The boundaries of financial reporting and how to extend them." *Journal of Accounting Research*, Autumn, 353-85.
» (1999) "Penetrating the book-to-market black box: the R&D effect." *Journal of Business, Finance, and Accounting*, April/May, 419-49.
» (1998) "The value-relevance of intangibles: the case of software capitalization." *Journal of Accounting Research*, Supplement, 161-91.

Goran Roos

Goran Roos is the founder of Intellectual Capital Services Ltd (ICS) and developer of its main concepts: determining value measurement, value and cost drivers, and strategic navigational issues. As a practitioner, he delivers the services of ICS to a wide variety of both private and public sector organizations around the world in a broad range of market segments.

Roos holds academic positions with the University of Queensland, Helsinki School of Economics, GEC Management College, and the Monash Mt Eliza Business School. He and his team are the authors and co-authors of numerous books and articles in the field of intellectual capital and strategy, and he serves on the editorial board of the *Journal of Intellectual Capital*. Roos was also named one of the 13 most influential thinkers for the twenty-first century by the Spanish business magazine *Direccion y Progreso*, No 167.

Roos developed intellectual capital mapping and valuation approaches that are used with managers to increase the value of the organization in the eyes of its stakeholders, articulate alignment of strategic intent, develop a disclosure policy as it relates to different stakeholders, provide knowledge transfer of leading edge know-how, and learn how to mesh and manage the value of intangible assets.

Roos has made major contributions to the field of intellectual capital by developing increasingly sophisticated tools, including the IC Index and the Holistic Value Added (HVA) approach for tracking changes in an organization's ability to transform resources to create value. The IC Index puts the emphasis on the transformations rather than the resources, which is how the value is actually created. This approach provides an authentic basis for value accounting, which allows an enterprise to account for value with all its constituent dimensions, as opposed to just accounting for the one dimension of cash. The more advanced HVA develops a complete measure that reflects the value perceived by any given observer/stakeholder.

Link
www.intcap.com

Highlights
Book:
» Roos, J., Roos, G., Dragonetti, N., and Edvinsson, L. (1998) *Intellectual Capital: Navigating the New Business Landscape*. New York University, New York.

Articles:
» (2000) "Towards improved information disclosure on intellectual capital," with A. Rylander and K. Jacobsen. *International Journal of Technology Management*, Summer.
» (1999) "The Knowledge Toolbox: a review of the tools available to measure and manage intangible resources," with N. Bontis, N.C. Dragonetti, and K. Jacobsen. *European Management Journal*, August.

Hubert Saint-Onge

Hubert Saint-Onge combines the most effective aspects of both a thought leader and a practitioner in the field. For over a decade, he has grappled with the issues of how to foster the transformation to sense-and-respond learning environments and entrepreneurial self-initiative in organizations.

Saint-Onge is senior vice-president for strategic capabilities, Clarica Life Insurance Company, a Canadian-based financial services firm. He was previously vice-president, learning organization and leadership development for the Canadian Imperial Bank of Commerce (CIBC).

Saint-Onge is implementing a corporate knowledge capital approach wherein value is created with each interaction that takes place between human capital, structural capital, and customer capital. For example, every time a staff associate interacts with a customer, that act will impact on the organization's customer capital.

Saint-Onge facilitates the leveraging of the firm's business through the systematic application of knowledge management and learning organization principles. The Knowledge Strategy that Saint-Onge forged provides the framework within which Clarica places new initiatives aimed at leveraging its intangible assets. The framework gives a context for growing those intangible assets through the exchange of knowledge, both within the organization as well as outside the organization with its business partners, and with its customers. It points to what it is trying to achieve and how Clarica will get there. It outlines the processes, the tools, and the infrastructure required for knowledge to flow effectively in a way that accelerates the development of capability. It delineates a phased approach, which takes into account the absorption capacity of the organization.

In addition, he has led an in-depth organizational effort to define the values and vision of Clarica to renew the development of the organizational culture in alignment with the strategic framework of the firm.

Links

http://knowinc.com/saint-onge/library
There are a number of articles and papers by Hubert Saint-Onge that can be accessed on the knowinc.com Website.
www.progressivepractices.com/publications.htm

Highlights

Article:

» (2000) "Conversation with Hubert Saint-Onge," with J. Chatzkel. *Journal of Intellectual Capital*, **1** (1).

Patrick Sullivan

Patrick Sullivan is a pioneering figure in developing the domain of extraction of value from intellectual capital. Since 1988, he has been helping companies extract value from their innovations. In his role as a senior partner of ICMG, Dr Sullivan specializes in helping companies focus on the integration of legal, business, and technology strategy to allow them to more effectively manage their intellectual capital.

Prior to founding ICMG, he was a testifying expert for Law and Economics Consulting Group, Inc., specializing in intellectual property valuations and litigation expert testimony.

As one of the founders of the ICM (Intellectual Capital Management) Gathering, Sullivan has been a catalyst for leaders in the intellectual capital movement and organizations involved with value extraction to share information and jointly develop decision processes, methods, and systems that effectively define, manage, and actively harvest the value of the latent intellectual capital resources.

Sullivan is closely associated with the ICM model of the knowledge firm, and has written several books on value extraction that explore how companies can practically develop and implement value extraction programs.

Link

www.icmgroup.com

Highlights

Books:

» (2000) *Value-Driven Intellectual Capital: How to Convert Intangible Corporate Assets into Market Value*. Wiley & Sons, New York.
» (1998) *Profiting From Intellectual Capital, Extracting Value From Innovation*. Wiley & Sons, New York.
» (1996) *Technology Licensing – Corporate Strategies For Maximizing Value*, with Russell L. Parr. Wiley & Sons, New York.
» (1999) "Extracting value from intellectual capital: policy and practice." In *Capital for Our Time*. Hoover Institution Press, Stanford, CA.

Articles:

» (2000) "Profiting from intellectual capital: learning from leading companies," with S. Harrison. *Journal of Intellectual Capital*, **1** (1).

» (1999) "Valuing knowledge companies," with J.P. O'Shaughnessy. *Les Nouvelles*, June, p. 83.

Karl Erik Sveiby

Karl Erik Sveiby is the founding father of the modern intellectual capital and knowledge-intensive organization movements. He is principal of his own consulting company, Sveiby Knowledge Associates, and an honorary professor at Macquarie Graduate School of Management in Sydney, Australia.

For the last 20 years, Sveiby has been working in, researching, consulting, and writing about "knowledge and business." He is the author of seven books, among which are *The New Organizational Wealth: Managing and Measuring Knowledge-Based Assets* and *Managing Knowhow*.

He began his explorations in 1979, trying to find out how to best manage the small publishing company with few tangible assets in which he was a partner. He found that while it did not have an abundance of traditional tangible assets, it did have substantial invisible knowledge-based assets, including excellent financial analysts, a well-known brand, and a large supporting network in the business community.

Sveiby is convinced that people are an organization's only profit generators, and that "human actions are converted into both tangible and intangible knowledge structures, which are directed outwards (external structures) or inwards (internal structures) ... These structures are assets because they affect the revenue stream." He defines these three areas of importance as: the competence of people; the internal structure; and the external structure. Various versions of the intangible assets monitor and the invisible balance sheet have been adapted by organizations around the world.

Sveiby came to see that his task was to create a toolbox to manage, measure, and cultivate knowledge-based assets. One major tool Sveiby created was the "intangible assets monitor" which allows managers to determine a firm's intangible assets.

Sveiby and Celemi, a Swedish-based company that creates learning processes, developed Tango, a business simulation model for the knowledge organization. Tango creates a hands-on experience of the interplay of the three areas of intangible assets as role players attempt to accomplish desired organizational outcomes.

Link

www.sveiby.com

Highlights

Books:

» (1989) *Den Osynliga Balansr "akningen Ledarskap* , w. "Konrad-gruppen." Outlines the first theory of measuring Intangibles. Available in an English translation as a PDF file, "The Invisible Balance Sheet."
» (1986) *Kunskapsf "oretaget,* ("The Knowhow Company") with Anders Risling. Liber, Malmo, Sweden.
» (1987) *Managing Knowhow,* with T. Lloyd. Bloomsbury, London.
» (1997) *The New Organizational Wealth.* Berrett-Kohler, San Francisco, CA.

Articles and published papers:

» (1992) "Strategy of the knowledge intensive firm." In: *International Review of Strategic Management,* Wiley and Sons, New York.
» (1996) "Knowledge organizations in Australia." Qbiz, Queensland University of Technology Australia (March).
» (1997) "The Intangible Assets Monitor." *Journal of HRCA,* **2** (1), Spring.
» (1998) "Measuring the wellspring of knowledge." *CPA Journal Australia,* June.
» (1999) "Designing business strategy in the knowledge era." In: *The Knowledge Advantage* (eds R. Ruggles and D. Holtshouse). Capstone, Dover, NH.
» (2000) "Measuring intangibles and intellectual capital." In: *Knowledge Management - Classic and Contemporary Works* (eds D. Morey, M. Maybury, and B. Thuraisingham). MIT Press, Cambridge, MA.

Resources

Intellectual capital is new to many people. Chapter 9 identifies excellent resources to visit for an extended introduction to the people, ideas, and major developments that are shaping the field:

» Websites;
» publications;
» intellectual capital books.

"Intellectual Capital is the currency of the new millennium. Managing it wisely is the key to business success in the knowledge era."

Nick Bontis, director, Institute of Intellectual Capital Research, Associate Editor, Journal of Intellectual Capital

CELEMI

Celemi is an international company, founded in 1986, with headquarters in Sweden. It serves three business areas: learning business, learning change, and learning marketing.

Celemi is a pioneer in the fields of intellectual capital and knowledge management. It has received the "MAKE" Award (Most Admired Knowledge Enterprises) for Europe and has been recognized as one of Europe's most dynamic, privately owned companies.

It has taken the principles and practices of being a knowledge organization to heart, using them internally as well as in the learning materials it offers. It uses the principle, espoused by Curt Nicolin, a leading Swedish industrialist, that "there's gold on the floor of our factories and we need to mine it now" to design learning tools to open communication channels, spread knowledge, and fire the motivation needed at all levels in an organization. The hidden assets of the organization come into play with its tools that foster active understanding and commitment. The outcome is developing the people, their strategies, and customer value.

Celemi worked closely with Karl Erik Sveiby to develop its tool, Tango, which helps organizations learn not only to measure, but also to manage their intangibles. It has applied the lessons from Tango to Celemi with its own Intangible Assets Monitor.

The Celemi Website contains a number of articles on capturing and leveraging knowledge value in organizations, applying performance measures, and management by learning.

Links

www.celemi.com

CFO.COM

CFO.com is a leading resource for senior financial executives on the Web. It provides news and articles on cutting edge practices to help keep top financial managers current and perform their jobs more effectively. The site also provides resources that help senior financial executives quickly access the relevant information on issues and opportunities.

Sister magazines include *CFO*, targeting US executives with financial responsibility, *eCFO*, a quarterly supplement covering finance and technology convergence in the US, Europe, and Asia, *CFO Europe*, and *CFO Asia*.

CFO.com has a repository of freely accessible articles, primarily on reporting aspects concerning intangible assets, but also some articles on strategic implications of intellectual capital management. Recent articles include an analysis of the US Federal Accounting Standards Board's controversial proposed changes in goodwill accounting rules that say companies do not have to amortize intangibles other than goodwill if they can prove that the assets do not have a determinable useful life. Another article, "Intangibles revealed," says that "over the next year [2001] companies could wind up spending some serious dollars to determine the fair value of intangibles and business units" which will be provided under the FASB new merger rules.

As the financial community begins to come to grips with the extensive growth in intangibles, accounting boards will be increasingly revising their standards, which will have substantial financial implications for organizations. Depending on the size and complexity of the business, this could entail valuation analysis that could cost from several hundred thousand to several million dollars. Having up to date information supported by analysis, with strategic implications clearly pointed out, will allow those with senior financial responsibilities to prepare themselves and their companies for the inevitable move to acknowledgment of intangibles as significant inputs into the valuation equation.

Link

www.cfo.com

ICMG

ICMG (Intellectual Capital Management Group) specializes in extracting value from innovation. Its Website reflects its interests in developing and growing competitive advantage through more effective management of a company's intellectual capital, its intellectual assets, and its intellectual property.

A good part of what ICMG does is education and on the Website ICMG maintains a bibliography containing books, conference presentations, white papers, and articles that are particularly germane to its mission. Many of the articles are by ICMG staff and others by thought leaders in their fields. These fields include intellectual capital (IC), IC management, intellectual property, knowledge management, and valuation.

The library is accessible by type of presentation and by field. The types of presentations are conference presentations, articles, white papers, and books. All materials, except books, can be downloaded. Abstracts of the books are online and the books are available for purchase.

The general areas these materials explore are: valuation, strategy, knowledge management, reporting, intellectual capital, intellectual assets, intellectual property, and human capital.

ICMG has more materials on value extraction than any other source and for that reason alone is worth knowing. Its other materials are equally valuable and make the site an ongoing and current center for learning.

Link

www.icmg.com

INSTITUTE FOR INTELLECTUAL CAPITAL RESEARCH

The Institute for Intellectual Capital Research, Inc. (IIRC) is a research think tank and consulting firm in the areas of knowledge management, intellectual capital, and organizational learning. The director of IIRC is Dr Nick Bontis, who is on the faculty at DeGroote School of Business, McMaster University in Hamilton, Ontario.

The Website offers access to a number of articles that Dr Bontis has authored which cover a range of areas involving intellectual capital, including an historical overview of the field, diagnosis and assessment of knowledge assets, conference and tool reviews, and case studies.

The IIRC site also maintains a links page for software and other tools important to the field and a corollary list of research and consulting organizations.

Link

http://www.business.mcmaster.ca/mktg/nbontis/ic/

THE INTANGIBLES RESEARCH PROJECT

The Intangibles Research Project is part of the Vincent C. Ross Institute of Accounting Research at New York University's Stern School of Business and is directed by Professor Baruch Lev.

Since valuation and disclosure issues related to intangibles are complex and little understood, accounting standard-setters around the world are encountering great difficulties in attempting to improve disclosures about intangibles. The "Intangibles Project" is designed for the exploration of the nature, measurement, and disclosure of the complete set of assets, tangible and intangible, which create value for shareholders. The project concentrates on internally generated intangibles, the most deficient area of reporting in meeting users' needs.

The project assists researchers in obtaining access to internal data on corporate intangible investments, and linking researchers with executives in charge of R&D, brand management, and human capital development for interviews, discussions, and exchange of information. The Intangibles Project also organizes meetings and conferences bringing together researchers, regulators, and executives to advance the investigation and implementation, particularly its annual "Intangibles Conference" at NYU.

The project's research and fact-finding reports create a ground of understanding and experimentation in the various aspects of intangibles and intellectual capital. The project explores issues such as: the private and social consequences of current ways of disclosing information about intangibles; how intangibles are valued by the financial and legal communities, as well as managers and others; experimenting with new intangible disclosure schemes; ways organizations classify intangibles; how accounting and disclosure work in different countries; and other problems and opportunities relating to disclosure, from a whole range of perspectives.

The project's Website maintains accessible information on its conferences and other events, as well as abstracts on case studies, capital market studies, productivity studies, and survey data studies.

Link
www.stern.nyu.edu/ross/ProjectInt/

JOURNAL OF INTELLECTUAL CAPITAL

The *Journal of Intellectual Capital*, established in 1999, is a quarterly journal focusing specifically on the management of intellectual capital. It brings together current thinking, research case studies, and experience. The *Journal* is a prime resource available to help academics, thought leaders, and practitioners create and manage a knowledgeable, coherent, and effective framework and set of practices for their organizations.

Contributors from around the world share their issues, strategies, methodologies, and approaches. The editorial advisory board is made up of many of the leading figures in the field, both academics and practitioners, who frequently provide articles on their new findings and work practices.

Journal coverage spans the full range of creating, extracting, and reporting intellectual capital activity. Articles cover intellectual capital as an economic discipline, looking into the business, legal, financial, and auditing requirements an organization might have. Secondly, they examine how to optimize the value of human, enterprise structure, and customer capital. They also explore tools, techniques, and processes used to identify, manage, and report intellectual capital.

The *Journal* is published in a print version, with the current and previous volumes accessible online through the publisher at Emerald Fulltext (www.emeraldinsight.com/ft).

Link
www.emeraldinsight.com/jic.htm

KNOW INC.

Know Inc. is a portal for a broad array of intellectual capital and knowledge management tools and methodologies. Its goal is to provide the intangible asset community with a workable framework for leveraging intangible assets. Although emphasizing knowledge management, Know Inc. can serve the valuable function of being a bridge between knowledge management and intellectual capital.

Know Inc. makes available a number of excellent articles and presentations by Hubert Saint-Onge and other leaders in the knowledge field. Additionally, it offers a series of toolkits co-developed with Karl Erik Sveiby, Hubert Saint-Onge, and Verna Allee, each of whom has extensive practical experience in this nascent field.

The portal design of Know Inc. will expand over time to allow it to be an enabler of a knowledge network, where practitioners, educators, and consultants can market the practices, methodologies, and tools that they have developed. Its Knowledgeshop makes available an array of books and other items in one space that make it easier to explore and select. It is a space where, increasingly, organizations can evaluate themselves, acquire the tools and professional assistance to assess and leverage their intangible assets, and share their learnings with the emerging knowledge community.

Know Inc. differs from most other knowledge service enterprises in that it offers both explicit, captured knowledge as well as opportunities to develop the social capital of a knowledge community. That makes it a worthwhile resource.

Link

www.knowinc.com

SKANDIA

Skandia, founded in 1855 as a property and casualty insurance company, has since 1991 transformed itself into a highly global insurance and asset management enterprise. An important enabler for that change has been the development of the intellectual capital perspective that Skandia has used to actively nurture, extract, and value its intellectual capital for over a decade.

Skandia's corporate Website (www.skandia.com) is the home of the materials and links that it has used to become a knowledge-intensive, innovative, globally networked enterprise. Many of these materials are accessible either as a download or for purchase.

The Skandia Website discusses the processes it implemented to develop its intellectual capital on a daily basis. It outlines how its customer capital, human capital, and organizational capital combine to create capability and value for the company and its stakeholders in ways that go beyond what a review of financial capital would reveal.

Skandia shows how, in the new economy, intellectual capital accounts for the major share of a company's total value. It demonstrates its intellectual capital management practices and a number of tools it created to visualize and report its intellectual capital.

Among these tools are: the Skandia Value Scheme, which shows the building blocks that make up its intellectual capital; the Skandia Navigator, a future-oriented business planning model; and the Dolphin, its PC-based business control software package, which is based on the Navigator. Skandia describes these in greater detail in a number of publications, on video and on CD-ROM.

The Website has the company's intellectual capital supplements from the years 1994–8 accessible for downloading. These publications review new developments and applications of Skandia's model for intellectual capital developed.

Hardcopies and CD-ROMs of various intellectual documents are listed and available for purchase on the site. The CD-ROMs are very imaginative and have videos and dynamic learning exercises embedded in them.

The Website also has lists of internal intellectual capital links as well as selected external links that are useful and provocative. The internal links are for the Intellectual Capital Community, the Skandia Futures Center and IC Visions, all of which are wholly owned subsidiaries of Skandia.

Links

www.skandia.com (go to Mission and Goals, and then to Intellectual Capital)

www.iccommunity.com

www.skandiafuturecenter.com

www.icvisions@afs.skandia.se

SVEIBY KNOWLEDGE MANAGEMENT

Karl Erik Sveiby provided the impetus for the current era of intellectual capital and knowledge management. Since the 1980s he has been "unlearning" existing management modes and "discovering" new ones. He has worked with organizations around the world to assist them in developing a knowledge-focused strategy, along with the ability to manage and monitor intellectual capital. His Website is a living repository of numerous articles that form a fundamental learning library for anyone involved in intellectual capital. The site has a basic introductory course to intellectual capital, as well as descriptions of the interactive tools he and his colleagues have developed to enable people to more effectively nurture and leverage their intangible assets.

All articles in the library are accessible and downloadable. They are primarily by Sveiby but also include pieces by other major contributors to the field. The library's major areas are: knowledge management and intellectual capital, the concepts of knowledge and information, managing knowledge organizations, measuring intangible assets, marketing and selling knowledge, and book reviews and bibliography.

The FAQ section is a composite of answers to the most frequently asked questions about the field. All responses fully recognize the value of the question and are extensive enough to provide a satisfactory basis to understand what can be an elusive topic.

Sveiby is constantly refreshing the site with updated and new materials. It is a great place to begin an intellectual capital journey, and start to understand the process of building a knowledge-based strategy.

Link

www.sveiby.com

CORE BOOKS

Adriessen, D. and Tissen, R. (2000) *Weightless Wealth: Find your real value in a future of intangible assets*. Financial Times/Prentice Hall, London.

Blair, M.M. and Wallman, S.M.H. (Task Force Co-Chairs) (2001) *Unseen Wealth: Report of the Brookings Task Force on Intangibles*. Brookings Institution Press, Washington, DC.

Botkin, J. (1999) *Smart Business: How Knowledge Communities Can Revolutionize Your Company*. Free Press, New York.

Brooking, A. (1996) *Intellectual Capital: Core Asset for the Third Millennium Enterprise*. International Thompson Business Press, London.

Danish Trade and Industry Development Council (1998) *Intellectual Capital Accounts: Reporting and managing intellectual capital*. Erhvervsfremme Styrelsen, Copenhagen.

Davenport, T.H. and Prusak, L. (1998) *Working Knowledge: How Organizations Manage What They Know*. Harvard Business School Press, Boston.

Davenport, T.O. (1999) *Human Capital: What It Is and Why People Investin It*. Jossey-Bass, San Francisco.

Davis, J.L. and Harris, S. (2001) *Edison in the Boardroom: How Leading Companies Realize Value from Innovation*. John Wiley & Sons, New York.

Davis, S. and Meyer, C. (1998) *Blur: the speed of change in the connected economy*. Warner Books, New York.

Dixon, N. (2000) *Common Knowledge: How Companies Thrive by Sharing What They Know*. Harvard Business School Press, Boston.

Devereaux, M.O'H. and Johansen, R. (1994) *GlobalWork: Bridging Distance, Culture & Time*. Jossey-Bass, San Francisco.

Edvinsson, L. and Malone, M.S. (1997) *Intellectual Capital: Realizing Your Company's True Value By Finding Its Hidden Brainpower*, Harper Business, New York.

Fitz-enz, J. (2000) *The ROI of Human Capital: Measuring the Economic Value of Employee Performance*. AMACOM, New York.

Friedman, T.L. (2000) *The Lexus and the Olive Tree: Understanding Globalization*, Farrar, Straus and Giroux, New York.

Imparato, N. (ed.) (1999) *Capital For Our Time: The Economic, Legal, and Management Challenges of Intellectual Capital*. Hoover Press, Stanford, CA.

Johansen, R. and Swigart, R. (1994) *Upsizing the Individual in the Downsized Organization: Managing in the Wake of Reengineering, Globalization, and Overwhelming Technological Change*. Addison-Wesley, Reading, MA.

Lev, B. (2001) *Intangibles: Management, Measurement, and Reporting*. Brookings Institution Press, Washington, DC.

Low, J. and Kalafut, P.C. (2001) *Invisible Advantage: Managing Intangibles and the Competitive Challenge*. Perseus, Forthcoming Fall 2001.

Stewart, T.A. (1997) *Intellectual Capital: The New Wealth of Nations*. Currency Doubleday, New York.

Sullivan, P.H. (2000) *Value-Driven Intellectual Capital: How To Convert Intangible Corporate Assets Into Market Value*. Wiley & Sons, New York.

Sveiby, K.E. (1997) *The New Organizational Wealth: Managing and Measuring Knowledge-Based Assets*. Berrett-Koehler, San Francisco.

Teece, D.J. (2001) *Managing Intellectual Capital: Organizational, Strategic and Policy Dimensions*. Oxford University Press, New York.

Ten Steps to Making Intellectual Capital Work

Being able to translate the ideas of intellectual capital into performance-enhancing actions and credibly gauging its value are what make an intellectual capital initiative worthwhile. Chapter 10 outlines key steps in developing a sustainable, value-adding intellectual capital program:

» think of your organization as a knowledged-based, intellectual capital supported enterprise;
» find the hook;
» map the organizational intellectual capital;
» set up initial measurements;
» make sure leadership buys in;
» build an active communication system;
» develop a supporting technology infrastructure;
» create opportunity zones for people;
» capitalize on created value;
» build the future now.

"The organization no longer has to rely on the executive suite to do its knowledge work. People throughout the firm can be asked, encouraged, and even required to think like a CEO."

Peter Drucker, organizational thinker and writer

While there is no single formula for making intellectual capital work in an organization, there is a perspective, reference points, and set of behaviors that enterprises can use to begin an intellectual capital process or initiative. The case studies in Chapter 7 show a variety of starting points and places of emphasis for intellectual capital efforts. The lesson is that anyone considering creating an intellectual capital effort should start with the particular needs of their organization.

Whether a company begins with an enterprise-wide view of its intellectual capital effort as a whole or it starts "where it feels the pain" or "can make the gain" can only to be determined on an organization-by-organization basis. Each company is different and operates with its own particular set of conditions. If there is an unprecedented strategic dilemma, as happened at Rockwell International, conditions may demand a laser-type focus on solving the specific critical issue. In other cases, a company with an extended history of dealing with intellectual capital issues may decide that the time has come to redefine how it is operating and make a strategic change, as was the case targeting intellectual property at Dow Chemical.

Factors that can play a role in both the decision to undertake an intellectual capital initiative, and the scope and shape of that initiative, are: the background of the enterprise, any special conditions that have emerged, the capabilities of the people involved, immediate and long-term goals, and the readiness of the enterprise to take on an initiative.

An intellectual capital initiative can be started proactively by an individual inside the organization, or it may be forced on a company by a convergence of external conditions. Regardless of the beginning circumstances, the ten points below give a set of navigation points for framing and implementing an intellectual capital process. Each organization may emphasize one cluster of points more than some others, but all will have a common need to build a basic set of capabilities and action principles.

1. THINK OF YOUR ORGANIZATION AS A KNOWLEDGE-BASED, INTELLECTUAL CAPITAL SUPPORTED ENTERPRISE

Instead of looking at your organization solely in term of its physical or financial assets, see the enterprise as a knowledge-based firm with an array of intellectual capital resources.

Start to think in terms of how mobilizing intellectual capital will be the enterprise's competitive advantage. Identify intellectual capital inputs that allow the organization to operate and track the degree to which they are embedded inputs into the firm's goods and services. Observe what people know, how they relate, and how they have infused their know-how into the organization and its products. This focus will reveal how an organization is created, innovations take place, processes happen, and revenue is generated.

A strategic knowledge-based view will expose how pervasive the role of intangibles is in the company. Pay attention to how these capabilities allow the organization to generate value. Look for areas where intellectual capital development and sharing are underutilized, ignored, or even impeded. The biggest gains from an intellectual capital program may come from opening lines of communication, discovering trading opportunities, and in cost savings. Notice also what intellectual capital has been cultivated by the organization or acquired by it so that it can achieve its strategic goals.

2. FIND THE HOOK

Gain the sponsorship of a senior leader in the organization who sees the need for this new perspective. Then, find out what particular performance problems people are having in the enterprise that can be solved by leveraging the organization's intellectual capital, either by cutting costs, generating revenue, or changing key relationships. This will enable buy-in and provide you with a legitimacy and a license to operate.

Make sure that these are the types of problem solving that you can show to the rest of the organization so that everyone can see that taking intellectual capital seriously is significant to their operations and future.

Start a network of other individuals in the enterprise who also see the need for an intellectual capital effort. Begin a shared learning process with these colleagues about the different dimensions of the field of intellectual capital and its ongoing developments.

3. MAP THE ORGANIZATIONAL INTELLECTUAL CAPITAL

Building on what was learned by people identifying their performance issues, comprehensively map where the stocks of intellectual capital are in the organization and how they flow throughout the enterprise to support achieving strategic goals. This will show where people are being supplied with the intellectual capital inputs they need to do their jobs and how they, in turn, transform those inputs into new and greater value for their customers. This will involve mapping people and their skill sets, processes, structures, and relationships. Be sure to include and utilize any databases that have already been developed in the mapping scheme.

Mapping will reveal where the system seems to be operating satisfactorily and where problem areas are. See "hot spot" problem areas as opportunity zones and places to start pilot projects that show the value of intellectual capital to the organization.

A small core group of people can carry out the mapping process with the aid of a network of individuals in the different operations of the enterprise.

4. SET UP INITIAL MEASUREMENTS

A sizeable number of measures and indicators are already in use in most organizations. Review them and determine which ones can show changes in performance tied with intellectual capital initiatives. Use these as trial measures initially, but over time develop a tested set of measures that the organization and individuals can deploy to navigate their fields and develop their capabilities.

These measures need to be revised and calibrated as needed to point out the extent of intellectual capital, and how it is being generated and used to support internal operations or turned into profits externally.

Since intellectual capital is composed of intangibles it is inherently difficult to measure them easily and precisely. In many cases, measures can at best tell if the organization is going in the right direction. Be careful to make sure that measurements are serviceable, that they warrant their cost, and that they do not take precedence over performance.

One reason for the demand for extensive measurements is that the concept of intellectual capital can be seen as hard to grasp. The more the concept is understood, the less the need to provide numerous measurements as proof of value. Using simple equations that are easily communicated, such as Rockwell's Value $= f$(intellectual capital $+$ financial capital), can go a long way to explaining the value of intellectual capital. As the organization comes to know how intellectual capital can be used, it is in a better position to choose an appropriate set of measures to guide and assess the organization's progress.

5. MAKE SURE LEADERSHIP BUYS IN

After the intellectual capital initiative is validated in pilot projects and its "better practices" begin to be shared with the different business units, the leadership of the enterprise needs to decide how, and to what extent, it will incorporate this new viewpoint into its strategies and navigation practices.

In one sense, as is shown in the Rockwell International and Clarica case studies, it may be best for leadership to have a limited, sponsoring role in the intellectual capital endeavor. However, they should be aware of its value and how they can nurture and best use the enterprise's intellectual capital for corporate advantage.

6. BUILD AN ACTIVE COMMUNICATION SYSTEM

Intellectual capital and its applications will be new to most organizations. Since people will be more likely to try what they know works, make sure that stories of the successful changes in performance are widely shared throughout the enterprise and, as appropriate, with suppliers and customers. A good story, told by word of mouth, may be the most powerful communication tool.

Another reason for an active communication system is that in the world of intellectual capital, people co-create wealth. Xerox's Eureka project (see Chapter 4) demonstrates how a group of technicians were able to develop and share their growing body of knowledge with each other globally, with great benefit to their colleagues, the corporation, and their customers.

Finally, intellectual capital is cultural. It is a living thing, not an artifact. It can only thrive where there are shared values, extensive trust, and active communication that support and enhance its growth.

7. DEVELOP A SUPPORTING TECHNOLOGY INFRASTRUCTURE

In contrast with financial or physical capital, intellectual capital can grow in value the more it is recycled. The more widely it is deployed, the greater the chances of it developing a critical mass of applications and user population. While a culture of collaboration enables the flow of knowledge in an enterprise, having appropriate technologies amplifies the speed, richness, and effectiveness with which intellectual capital can be accessed, used, and reused, as well as radically reducing costs of distribution. This facilitates the creation of a powerful intellectual capital capability.

An effective technology infrastructure supports all forms of communications, relational databases, analysis, and decision-making. Dow Chemical had a major advantage by virtue of its enterprise-wide database of its intellectual property. The ability to access that database was critical in deciding what intellectual property Dow would find it most advantageous to the company to retain, make available to the market, or let lapse.

Technology by itself is not the answer. People, not technology, create an organization's intellectual capital. Technologists and intellectual capital practitioners must, therefore, partner to design a people-centered infrastructure.

8. CREATE OPPORTUNITY ZONES FOR PEOPLE

Human capital is the core of intellectual capital. In the knowledge economy, with its flatter and increasingly virtual organizations, the trend is for people to be more related to their projects than their company.

The extended enterprise will need to form communities of practice with the broad mix of permanent employees, temporary employees, staff provided by suppliers, and even customers that come to make up its workforce. New levels of both leadership and management skills are extremely important to guide this hybrid workforce. Leadership must make sure to provide the context and create the opportunity zones so that its workforce will fully invest itself in achieving desired goals.

9. CAPITALIZE ON CREATED VALUE

Starting from the strategic vision of the firm and its stage of development, plan on how to grow, harvest, and extract value from the company's innovations, intellectual assets, and intellectual property. Determine how these intellectual capital resources will enhance the competitive position of the enterprise on a cost, revenue, or differentiation basis.

Chart the process steps for extracting value for the various forms of intellectual capital. Understand how conversion of human capital to structural capital can take place and be ongoingly leveraged by the organization. Identify the business units of the organization that are involved in generating intellectual capital and include key people from these as advisors on what and how its intellectual capital can be recycled across the organization, or marketed to the outside world.

The result will be an intellectual capital management system that the organization can use to capture, package, and leverage its critical know-how and convert it into structural capital for ongoing reuse. The organization will then have a reliable way to capitalize the value of its intellectual capital resources, ranging from its database management systems, manufacturing and sales automation tools, its array of intellectual property types (patents, trademarks, and copyrights), as well as other powerful intellectual assets, such as brand.

10. BUILD THE FUTURE NOW

Intellectual capital is the future of the organization. It must be nurtured systematically as a core competence so that the enterprise can continue to renew and develop itself. Companies need to start thinking 5–25 years into the future. The need is to visualize the kinds of skills, knowledge, process, communications, and technical competencies that will translate into the goods and services its customers will be seeking.

Think of the values, organizational structure, and relationships that have to be cultivated to support the development of those competencies. Exploring the future will also encourage rethinking of the present and promote the reshaping of the enterprise so that it becomes malleable enough to allow responses in unexpectedly changed conditions.

The time to begin building those competencies for the future is now. While no one can predict the future, the deep capabilities that are necessary to cope take time to develop. When done intelligently, the capacities that are created with an eye on future needs also give the enterprise a cutting edge advantage over its competitors in today's market, as well.

A RECIPE FOR SUCCESS

Starting an intellectual capital effort can be a scalable undertaking, in terms of both the numbers of its people and the amount of its budget dollars. If carefully defined and crafted, the initiative can accomplish a great deal. It needs to operate as if it were a recipe by bringing together the proper ingredients of an understanding of the field, committed people, the right skill sets, appropriate leadership support, and strong internal and external connections.

A good intellectual capital initiative, like a good recipe, does not happen in one swoop, but is shaped over time as the inputs are transformed. As the organization learns from its experiences and applies what it has learned in new experiments, it produces its next stage of capacities, structures, relationships, and directions. The steps outlined above are essential elements for an intellectual capital endeavor. Artfully include them for a successful outcome.

LEARNING POINTS

Ten steps to making intellectual capital work

1 Think of your organization as a knowledge-based, intellectual capital supported enterprise.

2 Find the hook.
3 Map the organizational intellectual capital.
4 Set up initial measurements.
5 Make sure leadership buys in.
6 Build an active communication system.
7 Develop a supporting technology infrastructure.
8 Create opportunity zones for people.
9 Capitalize on created value.
10 Build the future now.

Frequently Asked Questions (FAQs)

Q1: What is intellectual capital?

A: See Chapter 2, Section: User-based definitions.

Q2: Where in the organization can I find intellectual capital?

A: See Chapter 2, Section: From definition to framework for managing.

Q3: How do I carry out an effective intellectual capital program?

A: See Chapter 10, Ten Steps to Making Intellectual Capital Work.

Q4: Why has intellectual capital become so much more important recently?

A: See Chapter 1, Why Intellectual Capital is Important.

Q5: What are the origins of modern intellectual capital?

A: See Chapter 3, The Evolution of Intellectual Capital.

Q6: How do I find out more about intellectual capital?

A: See Chapter 9, Resources.

Q7: What is structural capital?

A: See Chapter 8, Section: Structural capital.

Q8: What are some organizations that have developed successful intellectual capital programs?

A: See Chapter 7, In Practice: Intellectual Capital Success Stories.

Q9: What are emerging issues concerning intellectual property?

A: See Chapter 6, Section: Intellectual property.

Q10: How can I use the Internet to market intellectual capital?

A: See Chapter 4, The E-Dimension.

Acknowledgments

The author would like to extend his thanks and appreciation to the creators and practitioners of the field of intellectual capital who have graciously shared their time, experiences, and hard-won knowledge, especially Hubert Saint-Onge of Clarica Insurance, Sharon Oriel of Dow Chemical, James O'Shaughnessy of Rockwell International, Patrick Sullivan of ICMG, Goran Roos of ICS, and Melissie Rumizen of Buckman Laboratories. The author is especially grateful to Barbara for her ongoing patience, support, and editorial insights.

Index